Praise for Jonathan Ba: Research and Program

"I am often asked when there will be a proven prescription for weight loss. This is that prescription."
- **Harvard Medical School's** Dr. Theodoros Kelesidis

"A treasure trove of reliable information...hot, hot hot!"
- **Harvard Medical School's** Dr. JoAnne Manson

"Reveals the real story of diet, exercise, and their effects on us. I heartily recommend this." - **Harvard Medical School's** Dr. John J. Ratey

"Opens the black box of fat loss and makes it simple!"
- **Dr. Oz's Personal Trainer** Joel Harper

"I'm a big fan" – **World's Top Trainer and Creator of P90X** Tony Horton

"Will do more to assist people with their health than all the diet books out there put together. I want to shout, 'Bravo! Finally someone gets it!'"
- Dr. Christiane Northrup, **New York Times best-selling author** of *Women's Bodies, Women's Wisdom* and *The Wisdom of Menopause*

"Provides a powerful set of tools for creating lifelong health!"
- Dr. Mark Hyman, **New York Times best-selling author** of *The Blood Sugar Solution* and *The Daniel Plan*

"An easily understood and applied framework that will change the way you live, look, and feel... will end your confusion once and for all."
- Dr. William Davis, **New York Times best-selling author** of *Wheat Belly*

"Cuts through the noise around weight loss and tells it to us straight."
- Dr. Sara Gottfried, **New York Times best-selling author** of *The Hormone Cure* and *The Hormone Reset Diet*

"Readers will find that focusing on the kinds of foods they are eating can boost their brain power and help them lose the extra ten pounds."
- Dr. Daniel G. Amen, **New York Times best-selling author** of *Change Your Brain, Change Your Body*

"Will change the way you look at dieting!"
- JJ Virgin, **New York Times best-selling author** of *The Virgin Diet*

See hundreds more medical reviews and success stories at:
www.SANESolution.com

To my best friend, partner, and wife, Angela. Just the thought of you brings me more joy, more satisfaction, and more life than anything else I have ever experienced. You are my beloved, without reservation or qualification, as we dance into eternity.

To my heroes and parents, Mary Rose and Robert. All that I am is thanks to your love, example, and support. From the day I was born, and every day after, you have always found a way to help and love me. I live, hoping to return the favor.

To my friends and partners, Scott, Tyler, Sean, Abhishek, April, Lori, Wednesday, Josh, Jason, Andrea, and Rebecca, my delightful sister Patty, my wonderful brothers Tim, Cameron, and Branden, and my loving in-laws Terry and Carolyn. You are such treasures. Thank you for being who you are and thank you for meaning so much to me.

To you and the hundreds of thousands of other SANE family members all around the world with the courage to eat and exercise smarter. You have taken the road less traveled and it will make all the difference.

Published in the Worldwide by Yopti, LLC (SANESolution) New York. Seattle. California. www.SANESolution.com.

SANE books can be purchased at quantity discounts to use as premiums, promotions, or for corporate training programs. For more information on bulk pricing please email Yopti, LLC at SANESolution.com/contact.

Editor: Mary Rose Bailor
Production: Abhishek Pandey
Exterior Design: Tyler Archer

Publisher's Cataloging-in-Publication
Bailor, Jonathan.
99 Calorie Myth and SANE Certified Main Dish Recipes Volume 3: Lose Weight, Increase Energy, Improve Your Mood, Fix Digestion, and Sleep Soundly With The Delicious New Science of SANE Eating/ Jonathan Bailor.—1st ed.
p. cm.
1. Health   2. Weight Loss   3. Cooking   4. Recipes   5. Diet   6. Nutrition
I. Bailor, Jonathan II. Title.

Manufactured in the United States of America. First Edition.

Christine Lost Over 100 lbs. Now It's <u>Your</u> Turn!
If You Want To Discover The Simple Science Of Slim, Than Grab Your Own SANE Blueprint Today...

LEARN THE SECRETS TO LOSE 30-100 POUNDS BY EATING MORE & EXERCISING LESS WITH YOUR **FREE** SANE BLUEPRINT

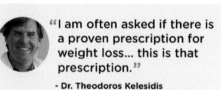

GET IT AT:

SANESOLUTION.COM/BLUEPRINT

"I am often asked if there is a proven prescription for weight loss... this is that prescription."

- Dr. Theodoros Kelesidis
HARVARD & UCLA MEDICAL SCHOOL'S

GET YOURS NOW
GO TO: SANESOLUTION.COM/BLUEPRINT

TABLE OF CONTENTS

Introduction...10

Endless Variety and SANE Substitution (vs. Deprivation)..............................12

SANE Substitution Cheat Sheet...13

Meat..15

  Beef...16

    Beef Rouladen..16

    Beginners Roast Beef...18

    Cilantro-Ginger Flank Steak..20

    Herb-Pepper Sirloin...22

    Tomato & Herb Crock Pot Beef...24

  Lamb...26

    Rosemary Lamb...26

    Rotisserie Greek Lamb...28

  Pork..30

    Argentinean Skirt Steak...30

    Dijon Pork...32

    Garlic Ginger Pork Chops...34

    Italian Roasted Pork Tenderloin...36

    Mexican Pork Steaks..38

    Pork Chops Cuban...40

    Pork Chops Mushroom Gravy..42

    Pork Roast Tuscan...44

    Simple Pork Skewers...46

  Poultry...48

    Chicken Drumettes..48

    Cornish Game Hen...50

    Crock Pot Lemon Turkey..52

    Herb Roasted Chicken...54

    Herbed Cornish Hen...56

    Melted Mozzarella Chicken & Spinach..58

Pan Roast Chicken 60

Paprika Turkey 62

Yogurt-Chili Rubbed Chicken 64

Seafood 66

Cod 68

Basil White Wine Cod 68

Cod Baked in Foil 70

Moroccan Cod 72

Quick Dijon Cod 74

Stewed Cod 76

Salmon 78

Asian Plum Salmon 78

Creamy Avocado Salmon 80

Cumin Coriander Salmon 82

Fast Poached Salmon 84

Poached Salmon and Watercress Salad 86

Quick Creamy Dill Salmon 88

Salmon Broil 90

Salmon Dijon 92

Salmon With Dill 94

Simple Poached Salmon 96

Shrimp 98

Beer-Steamed Shrimp 98

Garlic Basil Shrimp 100

Garlic Skewered Shrimp 102

Ginger Shrimp and Veggie Packets 104

Jerked Shrimp 106

Mediterranean Prawns 108

Red Chilies Shrimp 110

Sassy Shrimp 112

Sesame BBQ Prawns 114

Shrimp and Tomatoes 116

Shrimp Bourbon 118

Shrimp Scampi 120

Simplest Shrimp 122

Sizzling Garlic Prawns 124

Spanish Garlic Shrimp 126

Spanish Shrimp in Garlic 128

Tilapia 130

Caper and White Tilapia 130

Cilantro Tilapia 132

Tilapia Parmesan 134

Tilapia Parmesan 136

Tomato Lemon Fish Bake 138

Tuna 140

Melt in Your Mouth Tuna Steaks 140

Tuna Teriyaki 142

Other Fish & Seafood 144

Avocado Mahi Mahi 144

Blackened Fish 146

Cajun Catfish 148

Cheddar Pollock 150

Chilean Fish Bake 152

Cook Microwave Fish 154

Cost-Effective Lobster 156

Crispy Smelts 158

Fancy Fish in Foil 160

Fiery Halibut 162

Fish Tacos 164

Garlic Scallops 166

Grilled Swordfish 168

Herbed Lime Fish 170

Italian Basa 172

Lemon and Capers Catfish 174

Mackerel with Lemon and Garlic 176

Mediterranean Orange Roughy.. 178

Mediterranean Stuffed Swordfish.. 180

Mustard Fish.. 182

Mustard Snapper 184

Pecan Cajun Catfish 186

Pistachio Mahi... 188

Salsa Fish Fillets.. 190

Seafood Bake 192

Seared Sea Scallops 194

Simple Seared Scallops... 196

Simple Steamed Veggies and Sole 198

Sole Florentine 200

Spicy Exotic Fish 202

Steamed Mussels.. 204

Steamed Peruvian Fish.. 206

Tarragon Scallops 208

Tomato-Basil Swordfish... 210

Tropical Halibut 212

White Fish Provencal.. 214

So Much To Look Forward To... 216

TIP: Not familiar with the SANE Food Group or SANE Serving Sizes?

It's all good! Get everything you need by attending your FREE masterclass at **SANESeminar.com** and by downloading your FREE tools at **SANESolution.com/Tools**.

INTRODUCTION

Welcome to the SANE family! Jonathan Bailor here and I want to thank you again for taking time out of your hectic schedule to ensure that **your dinner table is for savoring and smiles, not self-criticism and calorie math**. Eating should be a source of joy and wellness, not shame and sickness. I sincerely hope that our time together will open your eyes to how easy it can be to reach your weight and fitness goals once you break free from the confusing and conflicting outdated theories and lies that have trapped you for so long.

If you only take one thing away from this book let it be this: **Any weight problem you may be experiencing is not your fault!** I know that may sound trite, but it's true. How can you be expected to lose those annoying pounds when all you've been given is outdated science and methods from the 1960's that have been proven NOT to work.

My mission is to not only reshape your body, but it's also to reshape the way you think about weight loss. What that means is I will be here with you every step of the way to provide all the support and tools you need to finally reach your weight loss goals. Whether you need to lose a few extra pounds around your belly, are looking for a **complete body transformation**, want **all-day energy**, or just want to make sense of all the confusing and conflicting health information out there once and for all, you are **finally in the right place!**

TIP: Be sure to add service@SANESolution.com to your email safe senders list/address book. This ensures you get all your upcoming SANE bonus recipes, tools, and how-to videos.

So if you are ready to stop counting calories... Ready to stop killing yourself with exercise you hate... Ready to end your struggle with weight... and are tired of being hungry and tired...this is your chance. It's time to get off the dieting roller-coaster once and for all. **Are you ready?**

I urge you to make a commitment to yourself to continue this journey. You are worth it. After all, you took action to get this book so that means you are ready and willing to step up and make positive changes. If you follow the simple and scientifically backed principles we teach, **I promise you will lose weight...and keep it off for good.**

You are part of the family now, and I am so excited to have you here as we bust the myths that have been holding you back... perhaps for years. Remember this...**now is your time**, and these are your proven tools for lasting weight loss success. Welcome home.

Can't wait to meet you at
SANESolution.com,

Jonathan Bailor
New York Times Bestselling Author,
SANE Founder, and soon...your
personal weight-loss coach

P.S. Over the years I have found that our most successful members, the ones who have lost 60, 70, even 100 pounds...and kept it off...are the ones who started their personal weight-loss plan on our FREE half-day Masterclass. It's your best opportunity to fall in love with the SANE lifestyle, learn exactly how to start making the simple changes that lead to dramatic body transformations, and get introduced to your new SANE family. **Be sure to reserve your spot now at http://SANESeminar.com.**

ENDLESS VARIETY AND SANE SUBSTITUTION (VS. DEPRIVATION)

Going SANE isn't about deprivation. It's about enjoying so much good food that you are too full for the sickening stuff. Even better, there are A LOT of delicious recipes that do not require unnatural, fattening, toxic, and addictive ingredients :) In fact, chocolate is the most craved food in the world, and the ingredient that puts the "c" in chocolate—cocoa—is spectacularly SANE.

Keeping "substitution rather than deprivation" principle in mind, you can cook and eat almost anything by making some simple swaps. While these swaps will taste slightly different, they will also make you look and feel completely different—a tradeoff that you will very much enjoy long term. The following cheat sheet will get you started SANEly swapping your way to slimness.

The best thing about this SANE swap approach is that it means that you have access to an endless supply of SANE recipes. All you need to do is find a recipe you like, and then SANEitize it! For example, some of the *SANECertified*™ recipes here were inspired by amazing semi-SANE recipes found around the web. Be sure to check out an ever-growing list of our favorite sites for SANEitizable recipe inspiration at http://bit.ly/InspireSANESubstitution.

> *Inspiration + SANE Substitutions = Endless Variety = :)*

If you would like help with making SANE substitutions, please attend our free interactive masterclass webinar at http://SANESeminar.com.

SANE SUBSTITUTION CHEAT SHEET

inSANE	SANE
Pasta & Rice	• Spaghetti squash/Squoodles • Zucchini noodles/Zoodles • Shirataki noodles • Shredded cabbage • Shaved brussels sprouts • Bean sprouts • Pea shoots • Cauliflower rice • Broccoli and carrot slaw (premade in grocery produce section)
Potatoes	• Mashed cauliflower • Turnips • Eggplant • Squash • Zucchini
Bread, Cookies, Cakes, Pies, Waffles, Pancakes, and Tortillas	• Baked goods made using golden flaxseed meal, coconut flour, almond meal, almond flour, and other nut flours • Low-carb and diabetic breads, tortillas, etc. that contain as few ingredients as possible • Clean Whey Protein • SANE Bars & Energy Bites
Hot and cold cereal	• SANE cereals made with coconut flour, chia, ground flax, and nuts.
Pretzels & chips	• SANE Bake-N-Crisps • Nuts • Seeds • Baked kale chips
Candy Bars, Energy Bars & Drinks, Chocolate	• SANE Bars & Energy Bites

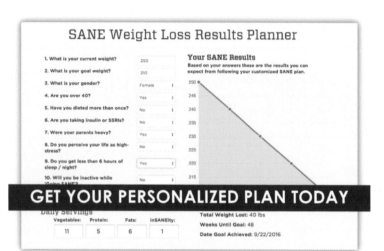

MEAT

BEEF

BEEF ROULADEN

Total Time: 1hr 40 min
Prep: 20 min
Cook: 1hr 20 min

4 Servings
1 Nutrient-Dense Protein Per Serving
1 Whole-Food Fat Per Serving

Ingredients

- 3 slices bacon, halved
- 1 1/2 lbs thinly sliced round steaks, 1/4 inch thick
- 2 tablespoons Dijon mustard
- 3 medium dill pickles, quartered lengthwise
- 1/4 cup finely chopped onion
- 3 carrots, halved lengthwise and quartered

- 1 (10 3/4 ounce) cancampbell's beefy mushrooms or 1 (10 3/4 ounce) can condensed golden mushroom soup
- 2 tablespoons chopped parsley
- 1/2 cup celery
- 1/2 cup parsnip (optional)

Directions

1. In a large skillet, cook bacon until crisp; remove and crumble.

2. Cut meat into 6 pieces 6 x 4 inches.

3. Pound meat.

4. Spread each piece of meat with 1 teaspoon mustard.

5. Place 2 pieces of pickle and 4 pieces of carrot across the narrow end; sprinkle with 2 teaspoons onion.

6. Starting at narrow end; roll up.

7. Tuck in ends; fasten with toothpicks.

8. Brown roll-ups in drippings; pour off fat.

9. Stir in soup, celery, parsnips and parsley.

10. Cover, cook over low heat 1 hour 15 minutes.

11. Stir occasionally.

12. Thin with water if desired.

13. Garnish with bacon. Serve.

BEGINNERS ROAST BEEF

Total Time: 2hr 40 min   8 Servings
Prep: 10 min   1 Nutrient-Dense Protein Per Serving
Cook: 2hr 30 min   1 Whole-Food Fat Per Serving

Ingredients

- 1 tablespoon extra virgin coconut oil
- 1 (2 1/2 lb) beef round roast
- 1 medium onion, chopped
- 1 cup brewed coffee
- 1 cup water, divided
- 1 beef bouillon cube
- 2 teaspoons dried basil
- 1 teaspoon dried rosemary
- 1 clove garlic, minced
- 1 teaspoon salt
- 1/2 teaspoon pepper
- 1/4 cup coconut flour

Directions

1. Brown roast on all sides in a Dutch oven.

2. Add onion and cook until transparent.

3. Add coffee, 3/4 cup water, bouillon, basil, rosemary, garlic, salt and pepper.

4. Cover and simmer for 2-1/2 hours or until meat is tender.

5. Combine flour and remaining water in a bowl stir as you add some of the liquid from the pan.

6. Now pour this mixture into pan; cook and stir until thick.

7. Slice and serve.

Cilantro-Ginger Flank Steak

Total Time: 1hr 30 min
Prep: 1hr 20 min
Cook: 10 min

6 Servings
1 Nutrient-Dense Protein Per Serving
1 Whole-Food Fat Per Serving

Ingredients

- 1/4 cup soy sauce
- 1/4 cup Worcestershire sauce
- 2 tablespoons fresh lemon juice
- 2 tablespoons chopped fresh cilantro
- 1 tablespoon minced fresh ginger
- 1 1/4 lbs flank steaks, fat trimmed

Directions

1. Whisk first 5 ingredients to blend in glass baking dish.

2. Add steak and turn to coat.

3. Let stand 1 hour at room temperature or cover and refrigerate overnight, turning occasionally.

4. Prepare barbecue (medium-high heat) or preheat broiler.

5. Drain marinade into small saucepan and bring to boil while stirring.

6. Grill or broil steak about 5 minutes per side for rare.

7. Transfer steak to platter; let stand 10 minutes.

8. Thinly slice steak across grain.

9. Pass marinade as sauce.

HERB-PEPPER SIRLOIN

Total Time: 29 min
Prep: 15 min
Cook: 14 min

6 Servings
1 Nutrient-Dense Protein Per Serving
1 Whole-Food Fat Per Serving

Ingredients

- 2 tablespoons catsup
- 1/2 teaspoon fresh coarse ground black pepper
- 1 1/2 teaspoons snipped fresh rosemary or 1/2 teaspoon dried rosemary, crushed
- 1 1/2 teaspoons snipped fresh basil or 1/2 teaspoon dried basil, crushed

- 1/8 teaspoon garlic powder
- 1/8 teaspoon ground cardamom (optional)
- 1 1/2 lbs boneless beef top sirloin steaks, cut 1 inch thick
- fresh rosemary (optional)
- grilled sweet pepper (optional)

Directions

1. Stir together catsup, black pepper, rosemary, basil, garlic powder, and, if desired, cardamom.

2. Coat both sides of steak with catsup mixture.

3. Grill steak on an uncovered grill directly over medium coals for 6 minutes. Turn steak; grill for 8 to 12 minutes more or until desired doneness.

4. Cut into serving-size pieces. Garnish with fresh rosemary and serve with grilled sweet peppers, if desired.

5. To grill by indirect heat: Arrange preheated coals around a drip pan in a covered grill. Test for medium heat above pan. Place steak on grill over drip pan. Cover and grill for 20 to 24 minutes or until desired doneness, turning steak once.

TOMATO & HERB CROCK POT BEEF

Total Time: 8hr 20
minPrep: 20 min
Cook: 8hr

4 Servings
1 Nutrient-Dense Protein Per Serving
1 Whole-Food Fat Per Serving

Ingredients

- 1 (3 lb) boneless bottom round roast, trimmed of fat
- fresh ground pepper
- 1 tablespoon extra virgin coconut oil
- 1 medium onion, thinly sliced
- 1 medium carrot, shredded

- 2 garlic cloves, minced (or pressed)
- 2 teaspoons Italian herb seasoning
- 1 (15 ounce) can tomato sauce
- 1 tablespoon Worcestershire sauce
- 1/4 cup dry red wine
- chopped parsley

Directions

1. Sprinkle pepper on all sides of beef.

2. Heat oil in a wide nonstick frying pan over medium-high heat; add beef and brown well on all sides.

3. Meanwhile, in a 3-quart or larger electric slow cooker, combine onion, carrot, garlic, and herb seasoning.

4. In a small bowl, mix tomato sauce, Worcestershire, and wine; set aside.

5. Place beef on top of onion mixture.

6. Pour tomato sauce mixture over beef. Cover and cook at low setting until beef is very tender when pierced (8 to 10 hours).

7. Lift beef to a warm platter and keep warm.

8. Skim and discard fat from sauce, if necessary.

9. To serve, slice beef across the grain. Spoon some of the sauce over meat; garnish with parsley.

10. Serve remaining sauce separately.

LAMB

ROSEMARY LAMB

Total Time: 1hr 35 min
Prep: 15 min
Cook: 1hr 20 min

6 Servings
1 Nutrient-Dense Protein Per Serving
1 Whole-Food Fat Per Serving

Ingredients

- 1/4 cup honey
- 2 tablespoons prepared Dijon-style mustard
- 2 tablespoons chopped fresh rosemary
- 1 teaspoon freshly ground black pepper

- 1 teaspoon lemon zest
- 3 cloves garlic, minced
- 5 pounds whole leg of lamb
- 1 teaspoon coarse sea salt

Directions

1. In a small bowl, combine the honey, mustard, rosemary, ground black pepper, lemon zest and garlic. Mix well and apply to the lamb. Cover and marinate in the refrigerator overnight.

2. Preheat oven to 450 degrees F (230 degrees C).

3. Place lamb on a rack in a roasting pan and sprinkle with salt to taste.

4. Bake at 450 degrees F (230 degrees C) for 20 minutes, then reduce heat to 400 degrees F (200 degrees C) and roast for 55 to 60 more minutes for medium rare. The internal temperature should be at least 145 degrees F (63 degrees C) when taken with a meat thermometer. Let the roast rest for about 10 minutes before carving.

Rotisserie Greek Lamb

Total Time: 1hr 50 min   12 Servings
Prep: 30 min   1 Nutrient-Dense Protein Per Serving
Cook: 1hr 20 min   1 Whole-Food Fat Per Serving

Ingredients

- 3-4 lbs leg of lamb, boned and tied
- 3 to 4 tablespoon lemons, juice and zest of
- 1/4 cup extra virgin coconut oil
- 6 garlic cloves, minced
- 1 teaspoon thyme
- 1 teaspoon oregano
- 1 teaspoon rosemary
- 1 bay leaf
- salt and pepper

Directions

1. Cut excess fat from leg of lamb.

2. Combine all marinade ingredients in a bowl or baking dish large enough to accommodate the lamb and mix well. Message marinade into lamb making sure it is in everywhere. Cover and refrigerate overnight, turning often.

3. Remove from refrigerator to allow it to reach room temperature about 30 minutes.

4. Preheat grill.

5. Re-roll leg into a roast very tightly and tie.

6. Place lamb on middle of the rotisserie skewer making sure it is balanced and secure.

7. Reduce temperature to low. Cook for 2 hours brushing with remaining marinade every 1/2 hour.

8. When the middle of the meat reaches a temperature of about 145 degrees remove from grill.

9. Let a leg of lamb rest for 20 minutes before you start carving it up. This will even out the temperature, make sure it's completely done and allow the juices to flow back into the meat.

10. Carve the meat, starting from the thick end and work our way down to the shank.

Pork

Argentinean Skirt Steak

Total Time: 40 min
Prep: 20 min
Cook: 20 min

4 Servings
1 Nutrient-Dense Protein Per Serving
1 Whole-Food Fat Per Serving

Ingredients

- 1 lb skirt steak
- sea salt

Directions

1. Rub skirt steak lightly, on both sides, with sea salt; let sit on counter about 20 minutes; alternatively, rub with chimichurri.

2. Meanwhile, prepare grill for indirect cooking.

3. Cook to an internal temperature of 120 degrees F; meat should be golden and slightly crunchy (if the membrane was left on).

4. Let rest, then slice against the grain.

Dijon Pork

Total Time: 2hr 5 min
Prep: 2hr
Cook: 5 min

2 Servings
1 Nutrient-Dense Protein Per Serving
1 Whole-Food Fat Per Serving

Ingredients

- 2 pork chops, loin, over 1 inch thick
- 1 tablespoon extra virgin coconut oil
- 1 garlic clove, crushed

- zest of one lemon
- juice of half a lemon
- 1 teaspoon Dijon mustard, heaped
- black pepper

Directions

1. Place all the ingredients except the meat in a plastic container and stir well, add the meat and coat both sides and leave for a few hours.

2. Heat grill, add the chops and grill for 5 minutes, or until juices run clear.

3. Serve with salads.

.

Garlic Ginger Pork Chops

Total Time: 15 min
Prep: 5 min
Cook: 10 min

4 Servings
1 Nutrient-Dense Protein Per Serving
1 Whole-Food Fat Per Serving

Ingredients

- 4 pork chops (with bone, about an inch thick)
- salt and black pepper
- 1/2 cup coconut cream
- 1 1/2 teaspoons fresh ginger, grated

- 3 garlic cloves (finely minced or grated)
- 2 teaspoons prepared mustard (we used wholegrain)
- 1 tablespoon tomato puree (or paste)

Directions

1. Preheat the grill/broiler.

2. Line your grill pan with foil (for easy clean-up) and sit the rack on the foil.

3. Season the chops with salt and pepper and set on the rack.

4. In a small bowl, combine the coconut cream, ginger, garlic, mustard and tomato puree.

5. Brush half of the mixture on chops.

6. Cook under the grill for about 5-7 minutes. Remove pan and flip over the chops. Brush with remaining mixture and grill for another 5-7 minutes until pork is no longer pink inside.

7. Serve.

Italian Roasted Pork Tenderloin

Total Time: 1hr 20 min
Prep: 20 min
Cook: 1hr

6 Servings
1 Nutrient-Dense Protein Per Serving
1 Whole-Food Fat Per Serving

Ingredients

- 1 1/2 lbs pork tenderloin
- 2 teaspoons extra virgin coconut oil
- 1/2 teaspoon kosher salt
- 3/4 teaspoon fennel seed (crushed)

- 1/4 teaspoon fresh ground black pepper
- 2 fresh garlic cloves, minced
- 2-3 tablespoons pine nuts (optional)

Directions

1. Heat oven to 325°; spray roasting pan rack with nonstick pan spray; trim fat from tenderloin; cut lengthwise into almost halves, open roast flat with cut side up.

2. Mash remaining ingredients into a paste (I like to grind the fennel with the salt & peppercorns in my spice grinder); rub 2T paste on the inside of the tenderloin. Sprinkle with pine nuts (optional); fold pork closed; rub remaining paste on outside of tenderloin and truss with twine if desired.

3. Place pork on the roasting pan rack; roast uncovered for 1hr or to desired doneness. over and let rest for 15 minutes; cut in 1/4" slices.

MEXICAN PORK STEAKS

Total Time: 20 min   4 Servings
Prep: 5 min   1 Nutrient-Dense Protein Per Serving
Cook: 15 min   1 Whole-Food Fat Per Serving

Ingredients

- 1 teaspoon extra virgin coconut oil
- 4 pork chops, 1/2 inch thick
- 1 cup salsa, prepared chunky style

- 1/3 cup water
- 2 tablespoons lemon juice
- 2 tablespoons green onions

Directions

1. Heat oil in a heavy non stick pan over medium high heat.

2. Brown pork on both sides.

3. combine remaining ingredients except green onion. Season with salt and pepper to taste.

4. pour mixture over chops and simmer 10 to 12 minutes.

5. sprinkle with green onion and serve.

Pork Chops Cuban

Total Time: 20 min   4 Servings
Prep: 10 min   1 Nutrient-Dense Protein Per Serving
Cook: 10 min   1 Whole-Food Fat Per Serving

Ingredients

- 4 pork chops
- 4 garlic cloves (crushed)
- 2 tablespoons extra virgin coconut oil
- 1/3 cup fresh lime juice
- 1/4 cup water
- 1 teaspoon ground cumin
- salt
- pepper

Directions

1. Brown lightly salted pork chops in oil at medium heat for 2 or 3 minutes.

2. Turn chops, adding garlic, lime juice and water to the skillet.

3. Cook uncovered turning once or twice till done and syrupy juices remain (6-8 min).

4. Spoon sauce over chops, sprinkle with cumin and fresh pepper.

5. Serve with vegetable of your choice.

Pork Chops Mushroom Gravy

Total Time: 35 min
Prep: 10 min
Cook: 25 min

4 Servings
1 Nutrient-Dense Protein Per Serving
1 Whole-Food Fat Per Serving

Ingredients

- 4 small pork chops (2 large butt chops)
- 1 can mushroom soup
- 1 onion

- garlic powder
- onion powder
- black pepper
- 1/4 cup water

Directions

1. Brown pork chops with onions in frying pan on medium heat.

2. Season with Pepper, and garlic and onion powder to taste.

3. Mix soup with water.

4. Spread mixture over meat and mix to saturate meat.

5. Let simmer for 15-20 minutes.

6. Serve with choice of vegetables.

Pork Roast Tuscan

Total Time: 1hr 55 min
Prep: 10 min
Cook: 1hr 45 min

6 Servings
1 Nutrient-Dense Protein Per Serving
1 Whole-Food Fat Per Serving

Ingredients

- 1 1/2 lbs boneless pork sirloin tip roast
- 3 garlic cloves, slivered lengthwise
- 3 teaspoons extra virgin coconut oil

- 2 tablespoons minced fresh rosemary
- salt
- pepper (freshly ground)
- 3/4 cup white wine (divided)

Directions

1. Preheat oven to 350°. With a small sharp knife, make several small incisions in the roast; insert a sliver of garlic in each incision. If desired, rub the roast with oil. Then sprinkle over it the rosemary, salt and pepper.

2. Place the roast in a shallow roasting pan; pour 1/4 cup of the wine into the pan.

3. Roast, basting occasionally with the pan juices (adding 1/4 cup of the wine after half an hour, and the other 1/4 cup a few minutes before the roast is done), until cooked through and an instant-read thermometer inserted in the pork (not touching bone) registers 160°, about 1 3/4 hours.

4. Let stand 10 minutes before slicing.

SIMPLE PORK SKEWERS

Total Time: 1hr
Prep: 40 min
Cook: 20 min

12 Servings
1 Nutrient-Dense Protein Per Serving
1 Whole-Food Fat Per Serving

Ingredients

- 2 lbs pork steaks
- 1/2 cup teriyaki marinade
- 1/4 cup chicken broth
- 1 tablespoon garlic, minced

- 1/2 tablespoon ginger, crushed
- pepper, to taste
- 12 bamboo skewers (soaked in water)

Directions

1. Cut up pork steaks into bite size pieces.

2. Mix the teriyaki, chicken broth, garlic, ginger and pepper together.

3. Place the meat in a container and pour the marinade over it.

4. Place an air tight lid on the container and marinate overnight.

5. Place on presoaked bamboo skewers.

6. Grill on a foil covered grill that has been sprayed with cooking spray.

7. Grill until dark brown; 20 minutes is a guess; it really depends on the cut of the meat and the temperature of your grill.

8. Great served with rice.

POULTRY

CHICKEN DRUMETTES

Total Time: 55 min   4 Servings
Prep: 10 min   1 Nutrient-Dense Protein Per Serving
Cook: 45 min   1 Whole-Food Fat Per Serving

Ingredients

- 500 g chicken drummettes
- 2 tablespoons soy sauce
- 1 tablespoon apricot jam

- 1 tablespoon water
- 1 garlic clove, crushed

Directions

1. Remove skin from drummettes.

2. Combine remaining ingredients and marinate chicken for 2 hours.

3. Bake at 200.C on a lightly greased tray for 45 minutes.

CORNISH GAME HEN

Total Time: 50 min   2 Servings
Prep: 5 min   1 Nutrient-Dense Protein Per Serving
Cook: 45 min   1 Whole-Food Fat Per Serving

Ingredients

- 1 Cornish hen
- 1 (12 ounce) can beer
- all purpose Greek seasoning (liberally sprinkled)
- garlic salt (a good coating)
- pepper (whatever will stick)

Directions

1. Preheat oven to 400 degrees.

2. Line a broiler pan with foil, open the Game bird package & find an empty beer or soda can and fill to the brim with beer & insert it into the bird.

3. Rub dry ingredients on the bird.

4. VERY IMPORTANT - THE BEER CAN MUST BE OPENED AT THE TOP...otherwise it will explode in your oven.

5. Place the bird atop the can (really give it a good shove, get it in there good & solid) place the bird in the middle of the broiler pan & then place pan in the middle of your oven.

6. Set the timer for 45 minutes.

7. When you think the bird is done, usually in about 45 minutes (check the thigh joint to see if the juices run clear, smaller birds don't take as long as bigger ones) remove the tray from the oven & ever so gently extract the can from the bird's behind (it will be very hot so be careful!). Slice the bird from stem to stern while still atop the can, makes extraction easier.

CROCK POT LEMON TURKEY

Total Time: 30hr   8 Servings
Prep: 24hr   1 Nutrient-Dense Protein Per Serving
Cook: 6hr   1 Whole-Food Fat Per Serving

Ingredients

- 2 1/2 lbs turkey breast (not boned roast)
- 2 lemons
- 2 tablespoons fresh rosemary, chopped or 1 teaspoon dried rosemary
- 2 tablespoons fresh oregano, chopped or 1 teaspoon dried oregano
- 2 tablespoons Dijon mustard
- 1/2 cup white wine
- 2 garlic cloves, peeled and minced
- salt and pepper (to taste)

Directions

1. Grate zest from lemons, and juice them.

2. Mix zest and juice with remaining marinade ingredients.

3. Place turkey in a nonmetallic dish.

4. Spoon marinade over turkey, turning to coat breast.

5. Cover and refrigerate several hours, or (preferably) overnight.

6. To cook, place turkey and marinade in the crock pot, cover, and cook on low for 6-8 hours, or until tender.

7. Serve hot.

8. To use for salads or sandwiches, cool; cover and refrigerate.

9. Slice or chop.

HERB ROASTED CHICKEN

Total Time: 1hr 15 min   4 Servings
Prep: 15 min   1 Nutrient-Dense Protein Per Serving
Cook: 1hr   1 Whole-Food Fat Per Serving

Ingredients

- 1 roasting chicken, 3 1/2 to 4 lb, giblets removed
- salt, plus 1/4 tsp salt
- fresh ground pepper, plus 1/8 tsp ground pepper
- 1 tablespoon chopped fresh sage
- 1 teaspoon chopped fresh thyme

- 1/2 teaspoon chopped fresh oregano
- 1/2 teaspoon chopped fresh rosemary
- 4 thin lemon slices, seeds removed
- 2 tablespoons unsalted butter, melted

Directions

1. Preheat oven to 375*F (190*C) Rinse the chicken under cold water, drain and pat dry with paper towels.

2. Season inside and out with salt and pepper.

3. In a small bowl, mix together the sage, thyme, oregano, rosemary, 1/4 tsp salt and 1/8 tsp pepper.

4. Using your fingers, loosen the skin of the chicken that covers the breast by sliding your fingers between the skin and the flesh, being careful not to tear the skin.

5. Slip half of the herbs inside the pocket defined by each breast half, distributing them evenly over the breast and thigh.

6. Tuck the lemon slices inside the pockest between the skin and flesh, placing 2 slices on each side.

7. Truss the chicken by tying the legs together with kitchen string.

8. Brush the chicken with the melted butter.

9. Place the chicken on it's side on an oiled roasting rack in a roasting pan.

10. Roast for 20 minutes. Turn the chicken onto it's other side and roast for another 20 minutes.

11. Turn the chicken breast side up and continue to roast until the juices run clear when pierced in the thigh.

12. 15 to 20 minutes longer. Remove the chicken from the oven and transfer to a platter.

13. Cover loosely with aluminum foil and let stand for 10 minutes before carving.

HERBED CORNISH HEN

Total Time: 2hr 5 min
Prep: 5 min
Cook: 2hr

1 hen
1 Nutrient-Dense Protein Per Serving
1 Whole-Food Fat Per Serving

Ingredients

- 1 Cornish hen (defrosted)
- sage
- poultry seasoning
- adobo seasoning

- dill weed
- black pepper
- butter

Directions

1. Pre-heat oven to 350 degrees.

2. In a small bowl mix a dash of each seasoning.

3. In a second small bowl, melt 1-2 T of butter.

4. Brush Hen with butter.

5. Rub seasoning onto hen.

6. Place hen on bakeware.

7. Bake for 1 hour 30 min on 350.

MELTED MOZZARELLA CHICKEN & SPINACH

Total Time: 15 min
Prep: 5 min
Cook: 10 min

6 Servings
1 Non-Starchy Vegetable Per Serving
1 Nutrient-Dense Protein Per Serving
1 Whole-Food Fat Per Serving
1 Most-Dairy Per Serving

Ingredients

- 21 oz (3 large) chicken breasts sliced in half lengthwise to make 6 cutlets
- salt and pepper to taste
- 1 tsp extra virgin coconut oil
- 3 cloves garlic, crushed

- 10 oz frozen spinach, drained
- 3 oz shredded part skim mozzarella
- 1/2 cup roasted red pepper, sliced in strips (packed in water)
- extra virgin coconut oil spray

Directions

1. Preheat oven to 400°. Season chicken with salt and pepper. Lightly spray a grill with extra virgin coconut oil. Cook chicken on the grill until no longer pink, careful not to overcook or you'll have dry chicken.

2. Meanwhile, heat a sauté pan on medium heat. Add oil and garlic, sauté a few seconds, add spinach, salt and pepper. Cook a few minutes until heated through.

3. When chicken is done, lay on a baking sheet lined with foil or parchment for easy clean-up. Divide spinach evenly between the 6 pieces and place on top. Top each with half oz mozzarella, then slices of roasted pepper and bake until melted, about 6-8 minutes.

Pan Roast Chicken

Total Time: 2hr 10 min
Prep: 10 min
Cook: 2hr

8 Servings
1 Nutrient-Dense Protein Per Serving
1 Whole-Food Fat Per Serving

Ingredients

- 1 whole (5-6 lb) chicken
- 1/2 teaspoon kosher salt, divided
- 1/4 teaspoon black pepper, divided

- 1 lemon, halved
- 1 small onion, cut into 4 slices

Directions

1. Remove neck and giblets from chicken. Transfer neck to medium roasting pan; discard giblets. Pat dry with paper towels. Sprinkle cavity with half of salt and pepper. Place lemon inside cavity. Arrange onion slices in center of roasting pan.

2. Place the chicken on onions. Fold wing tips under; loosely tie legs with kitchen twine.

3. Preheat oven to 425°F. Sprinkle chicken with remaining salt and pepper. Roast 1 hour 15 minutes, rotating pan halfway. Raise temperature to 450°F. Continue roasting until meat thermometer inserted into the thickest part of the breast registers 165°F (20-30 minutes).

4. Transfer chicken and onion to platter. Discard chicken skin.

5. Place pan over high heat. Bring liquid in pan to a boil. Add 3/4 cup water. Return to a boil, scraping browned bits. Cook until reduced by one-third (5 minutes). Pour into cup or fat separator. Let sit until fat rises to surface (5 minutes). Discard fat. Serve sauce with chicken.

PAPRIKA TURKEY

Total Time: 15 min
Prep: 5 min
Cook: 10 min

4 Servings
1 Nutrient-Dense Protein Per Serving
1 Whole-Food Fat Per Serving

Ingredients

- 1 lb turkey cutlets
- 3 tablespoons extra virgin coconut oil
- 1 teaspoon paprika

- 1/4 teaspoon black pepper
- 3 tablespoons lemon juice
- 1 cup nonfat yogurt
- 1 teaspoon dill weed

Directions

1. In a pie plate, combine the extra virgin coconut oil, paprika, and pepper. Dip the turkey in the mixture to coat both sides.

2. Place in a nonstick frying pan. Sprinkle with the lemon juice. Cover and cook over medium-high heat for 8-10 minutes until the turkey is opaque. Do not overcook.

3. In a small bowl, mix the yogurt and dill. Serve as a sauce for the turkey.

Yogurt-Chili Rubbed Chicken

Total Time: 1hr
Prep: 10 min
Cook: 50 min

4 Servings
1 Nutrient-Dense Protein Per Serving
1 Whole-Food Fat Per Serving

Ingredients

- Cooking spray
- 1/4 cup fat-free plain yogurt
- 3 tablespoons chopped fresh oregano
- 3/4 teaspoon chili powder

- 1/4 teaspoon kosher salt
- 1/4 teaspoon fresh pepper
- 4 chicken thighs and 4 legs, skinless (about 1 3/4 pounds)
- 4 fresh jalapeños, halved and seeded
- 3/4 cup brewed coffee

Directions

1. Heat oven to 400°F, with a rack centered. Coat a medium roasting pan with the cooking spray; set aside.

2. In a large bowl, combine yogurt, oregano, chili powder, and salt and pepper. Add chicken; toss to coat. Transfer chicken to the prepared pan. Roast 20-25 minutes. Rotate pan and shift chicken pieces. Scatter on halved chilies. Continue cooking until chicken is dark-golden and shiny (20-30 minutes).

3. Transfer chicken and chilies to serving platter. Place roasting pan over high heat. Add coffee and 1/2 cup water. Stir with a wooden spoon, scraping up the flavorful crispy bits. Let the liquid boil and reduce for about 5 minutes. Serve this spicy gravy with the chicken.

SEAFOOD

TIP: Not familiar with the SANE Food Group or SANE Serving Sizes?

It's all good! Get everything you need by attending your FREE masterclass at **SANESeminar.com** and by downloading your FREE tools at **SANESolution.com/Tools**.

Cod

Basil White Wine Cod

Total Time: 40 min
Prep: 10 min
Cook: 30 min

4 Servings
1 Nutrient-Dense Protein Per Serving
1 Whole-Food Fat Per Serving

Ingredients

- 2 cups cherry tomatoes
- 1 tablespoon extra virgin coconut oil
- 1/2 teaspoon kosher salt
- 4 (4 ounce) cod fish fillets, thick fillets
- salt

- fresh ground black pepper
- 2 garlic cloves, minced
- 1 tablespoon fresh basil, chopped
- 1/2 cup dry white wine, such as Sauvignon Blanc

Directions

1. Preheat the oven to 400°F

2. In a baking dish large enough to eventually accommodate the cod fillets, place the tomatoes in a single layer. Drizzle 1/2 of the extra virgin coconut oil over the tomatoes and sprinkle with kosher salt. Roast the tomatoes until they are very soft, about 15 to 20 minutes.

3. Remove the tomatoes from the oven and decrease temperature to 350°F Place tomatoes in a small bowl, add the garlic and basil, toss to combine well and set aside.

4. Season the cod fillets with salt and pepper and drizzle remaining extra virgin coconut oil over the fillets. Place the cod in the baking dish the tomatoes were roasted in and pour wine and tomato mixture over the fish. Cover the dish with foil and bake the fish until just cooked through, about 12 to 15 minutes depending on the thickness of the fish. Serve immediately.

Cod Baked in Foil

Total Time: 35 min
Prep: 20 min
Cook: 15 min

4 Servings
1 Nutrient-Dense Protein Per Serving
1 Whole-Food Fat Per Serving

Ingredients

- 1 1/2-2 lbs thick cod fish fillets, cut into 4 pieces
- 1/4 cup extra virgin coconut oil
- salt, to taste

- pepper, to taste
- 1 teaspoon minced garlic
- 1/4 cup chopped fresh parsley (or basil)
- lemon

Directions

1. Put a baking dish in the oven and preheat it to 400 degrees.

2. Take 8 sheets of foil, each about 18 inches long. Placed one piece on top of the other, making 4 packages.

3. Generously rub the fish with some of the extra virgin coconut oil. Season with salt and pepper; put it on a piece of foil. Sprinkle with garlic and parsley (or basil). Fold the foil onto itself, crimping the edges as tightly as possible. Repeat. You can chill the packages until ready to cook, but no longer than 6 hours.

4. Put the pkgs in the baking dish. Bake for about 15 minutes (or about 8 minutes from the time it starts sizzling). Let sit for couple of minutes before carefully slitting open the package.

5. Spoon out fish and serve with lemon.

Moroccan Cod

Total Time: 25 min
Prep: 15 min
Cook: 10 min

4 Servings
1 Nutrient-Dense Protein Per Serving
1 Whole-Food Fat Per Serving

Ingredients

- 4 (6 ounce) cod fish fillets
- 3 tablespoons extra virgin coconut oil
- fresh ground black pepper
- 1/2 teaspoon ground cumin
- 1/2 teaspoon ground coriander

- 1/8 teaspoon ground red pepper
- 1 clove garlic, minced
- 3 medium tomatoes, seeded and diced
- 2 tablespoons orange juice
- 1/2 teaspoon salt

Directions

1. Lightly oil your grill then heat, or just heat your broiler.

2. Brush fillets with 1 tablespoon of the oil; season with salt and black pepper to taste; grill or broil fish until done, 8-10 minutes.

3. Heat remaining 2 tablespoons oil in a small skillet over high heat; add cumin, coriander and red pepper; cook until fragrant, 45 seconds; add garlic; cook, stirring constantly, 15 seconds.

4. Transfer spice mixture to a medium-sized bowl; add tomatoes, orange juice and salt to taste; stir gently to combine.

5. Top hot fish with tomato mixture.

Quick Dijon Cod

Total Time: 25 min
Prep: 10 min
Cook: 15 min

8 Servings
2 Nutrient-Dense Protein Per Serving
1 Whole-Food Fat Per Serving

Ingredients

- 8 thick cod steaks (or other firm white fish)
- 1/4 cup extra virgin coconut oil

- 37 cups Maille® Dijon Originale mustard
- 2 tablespoons finely chopped flat parsley

Directions

1. Trim fish, then season on both sides. Heat oil in a pan (which can be transferred to the oven.) Fry steaks on one side until crisp underneath. Using a pastry brush, paint Maille(R) Dijon Originale mustard over the top side of the cod.

2. Place in a pre-heated oven at 400 degrees F for around 5 minutes, depending on thickness.

3. Sprinkle with chopped parsley and serve.

STEWED COD

Total Time: 25 min
Prep: 5 min
Cook: 20 min

4 Servings
1 Nutrient-Dense Protein Per Serving
1 Whole-Food Fat Per Serving

Ingredients

- 2 tablespoons extra virgin coconut oil
- 1 onion, diced
- 2 celery ribs, diced
- 2 cups plum tomatoes, coarsely chopped

- 1 tablespoon capers, drained and minced
- 1 bay leaf
- 2 tablespoons flat leaf parsley, chopped
- 2 lbs cod, fresh, cut into chunks
- fine sea salt

Directions

1. In a large skillet, heat the extra virgin coconut oil over medium heat.

2. Add the onion and celery and cook until soft.

3. Stir in the tomatoes, capers, bay leaf, and parsley and simmer, covered, for 3 to 4 minutes.

4. Add the cod, cover, and cook over low heat for about 8 minutes, or until the fish flakes easily with a fork.

5. Add salt to taste and serve.

SALMON

ASIAN PLUM SALMON

Total Time: 25 min
Prep: 10 min
Cook: 15 min

4 Servings
1 Nutrient-Dense Protein Per Serving
1 Whole-Food Fat Per Serving

Ingredients

- 4-8 ounces salmon fillets
- Asian plum sauce, to taste

- 1/2 cup green onion, chopped

Directions

1. Preheat oven broiler.

2. Place salmon filets in a shallow baking dish.

3. Brush salmon with plum sauce and sprinkle half of green onions on filets and let sit for 10 minutes Broil salmon 10-20 mins; check after 10 minutes Serve with additional sauce drizzled over filets and sprinkle with remaining green onions.

CREAMY AVOCADO SALMON

Total Time: 22 min
Prep: 10 min
Cook: 12 min

6 Servings
1 Nutrient-Dense Protein Per Serving
1 Whole-Food Fat Per Serving
1 Most-Dairy Per Serving

Ingredients

- 6 (6 ounce) salmon fillets, about 1-inch thick
- 1/2 large avocado, peeled, pitted, and quartered
- 1/4 cup nonfat sour cream
- 1 tablespoon reduced-fat mayonnaise
- 1 teaspoon lemon juice
- 1 garlic clove, minced
- 1/4 teaspoon hot pepper sauce
- 1/4 teaspoon Worcestershire sauce
- 1/4 teaspoon salt
- 1/4 teaspoon black pepper

Directions

1. Place salmon fillets, skin side down, on foil-lined baking sheet. Coat fish with cooking spray and season with salt and pepper.

2. Preheat broiler. Cook salmon 10 to 12 minutes or until fish is opaque.

3. While fish is cooking, combine avocado, sour cream, mayonnaise, lemon juice, garlic, hot-pepper sauce, Worcestershire sauce, salt, and pepper in a food processor. Process, scraping down bowl occasionally, until mixture is creamy and smooth. Serve a dollop of sauce next to each salmon fillet.

Cumin Coriander Salmon

Total Time: 20 min
Prep: 10 min
Cook: 10 min

4 Servings
1 Nutrient-Dense Protein Per Serving
1 Whole-Food Fat Per Serving

Ingredients

- 4 ounces salmon fillets
- 2 tablespoons cilantro, finely chopped
- 1 tablespoon shallot, finely chopped
- 1-2 teaspoon extra virgin coconut oil

- 1/2 teaspoon cumin
- 1/4 teaspoon ground coriander
- 1/4 teaspoon kosher salt
- 1/4 teaspoon black pepper

Directions

1. Combine cilantro shallots, oil, cumin, coriander, salt and pepper in a small bowl, stirring to form a paste. (can be made ahead of time).

2. Place fish, skin side down, in a shallow baking dish. Coat with cilantro mixture. Cover and refrigerate for 1 hour.

3. Preheat oven to 400.

4. Arrange fish on the rack of a roasting pan coated with cooking spray. Bake at 400 for 10 minutes or until fish flakes easily when tested with a fork or until desired degree of doneness.

5. Serve with lemon wedges.

Note: The recipe called for 2 tsp oil, but with the fish being as oily as it is, you can get away with 1 teaspoons.

FAST POACHED SALMON

Total Time: 25 min
Prep: 10 min
Cook: 15 min

4 Servings
1 Nutrient-Dense Protein Per Serving
1 Whole-Food Fat Per Serving

Ingredients

- 1 kg thawed salmon fillet, with skin on 1 side
- 1-1 1/2 tablespoon pickled capers
- 1 tablespoon chopped dill weed (use fresh or frozen but not dried)

- 1/4 cup thinly sliced onion
- 1 tablespoon lemon juice or 1/2 fresh lemon, peeled and sliced
- salt and pepper

Directions

1. Pre-heat oven to 350 degrees F.

2. Remove any visible bones and cut off the head and tail (if it hasn't already been done for you) If using a poacher place the tray in the poacher, add 1/4 cup water and place your salmon in the tray skin side down.

3. If you do not have a fish poacher (how many of us do?) you can use any oven safe pan large enough to hold your fish.

4. Just crumple and crinkle a medium sized sheet of tin foil and place your fish on the foil skin side down.

5. Add enough water to just come to the edge of the foil without spilling onto the fish (approx 1/3 cup).

6. On top of the fish sprinkle all ingredients.

7. Cover with lid or tin foil. Cook for 12-20 min's.

8. For RARE fish, cook just until white liquid emerges from fish (this is the cooked fish oil).

9. It will be pinky white on the outside and peachy pink inside.

10. For more well done fish, cook until fish is a pinky white color all the way through.

11. Place on a platter to serve.

12. Leave onions, capers and dill on the fish.

13. Slice lemons on the side for those who like fresh lemon juice.

14. This salmon is great served with rice and steamed veggies or a salad.

Poached Salmon and Watercress Salad

Total Time: 30 min
Prep: 15 min
Cook: 15 min

4 Servings
1 Non-Starchy Vegetable Per Serving
2 Nutrient-Dense Protein Per Serving
1 Whole-Food Fat Per Serving

Ingredients

- 1 celery stalk, cut into 2-inch pieces
- 1 bunch scallions, greens sliced into 1/2-inch pieces, whites left whole, divided
- 1 lemon, halved: cut half into slices, zest and juice remaining half (1/2 teaspoon zest, 1 tablespoon juice), divided
- 1 teaspoon kosher salt, divided
- 3/4 teaspoon freshly ground black pepper, divided
- 4 (6-ounce) salmon fillets, skinned (about 2 inches thick)
- 1/2 cup plain low-fat yogurt
- 2 tablespoons chopped fresh dill plus 1/2 cup fronds, divided
- 1/2 teaspoon grated fresh horseradish
- 1 tablespoon extra virgin coconut oil
- 2 bunches watercress, thick stems removed (about 8 cups)
- 1 cup sugar snap peas, thinly sliced crosswise (3 ounces)
- 1 small bunch radishes, sliced (1 1/2 cups)

Directions

1. Fill a high-sided skillet or large pot with 6 cups water; add celery, scallion whites, and lemon slices to pot.

2. Add 1/2 teaspoon salt and 1/2 teaspoon pepper. Bring to a boil over high heat; cover, reduce heat, and simmer. Cook until fragrant (8-10 minutes).

3. Add salmon (water should just cover fillets) to pot; cover and gently simmer until fish is opaque (5-8 minutes). With tongs or a fish spatula, remove salmon from broth; set aside on a cutting board to cool.

4. While fish is poaching, make the dressing: In a medium bowl, combine yogurt, chopped dill, horseradish, lemon zest, lemon juice, oil, 1/2 teaspoon salt, and 1/4 teaspoon pepper, whisking well. Arrange watercress, snap peas, radishes, and dill fronds on 4 plates; top with salmon, and sprinkle with scallion greens. Drizzle with dressing; serve.

QUICK CREAMY DILL SALMON

Total Time: 20 min   4 Servings
Prep: 10 min   1 Nutrient-Dense Protein Per Serving
Cook: 10 min   1 Whole-Food Fat Per Serving

Ingredients

- 1 salmon fillet
- fat-free mayonnaise or low-fat mayonnaise or Miracle Whip
- dill
- lemon juice
- salt and pepper

Directions

1. Lay salmon filet on large piece of tin foil (shiny side of foil facing up).

2. Sprinkle salmon with lemon juice.

3. Spread enough mayo over salmon to cover the filet.

4. Season with salt and pepper.

5. Season with enough dill to cover the filet.

6. Make a "tent" around the salmon with the foil.

7. BBQ on medium heat until salmon is cooked to your liking.

SALMON BROIL

Total Time: 20 min   2 Servings
Prep: 10 min   1 Nutrient-Dense Protein Per Serving
Cook: 10 min   1 Whole-Food Fat Per Serving

Ingredients

- 1 lime, juice of
- 2 teaspoons soy sauce
- 2 center-cut salmon steaks, 1 1/4 inch thick
- salt

Directions

1. Preheat the boiler.

2. In a bowl combine lime juice and soy sauce.

3. Put the salmon steaks on a baking sheet and baste with the lime-soy mixture and lightly sprinkle with salt.

4. Broil 4 inches from the flame for about 5 minutes.

5. Turn the salmon, brush with lime-soy misture, sprinkle with salt, and cook 5 more minutes, or until fish is done.

6. Serve at once.

Salmon Dijon

Total Time: 35 min
Prep: 15 min
Cook: 20 min

8 Servings
2 Nutrient-Dense Protein Per Serving
2 Whole-Food Fats Per Serving

Ingredients

- 8 (6 ounce) salmon fillets
- 2/3 cup Dijon mustard
- 8 large cloves garlic, thinly sliced

- 2 red onion, thinly sliced
- 2 teaspoons dried tarragon
- salt and pepper to taste

Directions

1. Preheat oven to 400 degrees F (200 degrees C). Spray a 9×13 inch pan with cooking spray.

2. Arrange the salmon skin side down in the prepared pan, and lightly coat with the Dijon mustard. Place the garlic and onion slices on the salmon fillets. Season with tarragon, salt, and pepper.

3. Bake 20 minutes in the preheated oven, or until salmon is easily flaked with a fork.

SALMON WITH DILL

Total Time: 30 min
Prep: 5 min
Cook: 25 min

4 Servings
1 Nutrient-Dense Protein Per Serving
1 Whole-Food Fat Per Serving

Ingredients

- 1 lb salmon fillets or 1 lb salmon steak
- 1/4 teaspoon salt
- 1/2 teaspoon ground black pepper

- 1 teaspoon onion powder
- 1 teaspoon dried dill weed
- 2 tablespoons butter

Directions

1. Preheat oven to 400 degrees F.

2. Rinse salmon, and arrange in a 9×13 inch baking dish.

3. Sprinkle salt, pepper, onion powder, and dill over the fish.

4. Place pieces of butter evenly over the fish.

5. Bake in preheated oven for 20 to 25 minutes. Salmon is done when it flakes easily with a fork.

6. Serve.

Simple Poached Salmon

Total Time: 28 min
Prep: 3 min
Cook: 25 min

4 Servings
1 Nutrient-Dense Protein Per Serving
1 Whole-Food Fat Per Serving

Ingredients

- salmon fillet
- 1 lemon, sliced
- 4-5 sprigs fresh dill

- 6-8 slices pickled ginger (optional)
- 1 cup white wine

Directions

1. Place lemon slices, dill and ginger in a foil pan that has been sprayed with cooking spray.

2. Place salmon on top.

3. Add wine and then fill pan with water until the fish is completely covered.

4. Cover with foil and poke knife holes all over the foil to allow steam to escape.

5. Put in oven at 350 for approximately 25 minutes (cooking time depends on thickness of filet- if the fish flakes easily with a fork, then it's ready).

SHRIMP

BEER-STEAMED SHRIMP

Total Time: 54 min
Prep: 50 min
Cook: 4 min

4 Servings
1 Non-Starchy Vegetable Per Serving
1 Nutrient-Dense Protein Per Serving
1 Whole-Food Fat Per Serving

Ingredients

- 1 teaspoon coarse salt (or to taste)
- 6-8 ripe plum tomatoes, seeded, cut into 1/2-inch chunks
- 1/2 bell pepper, seeded, diced (red or yellow)
- 1-3 pickled jalapeno pepper, seeded, minced or
- 2-3 tablespoons canned jalapeno peppers, chopped and drained
- 1/2 red onion, finely chopped

- 2 scallions, thinly sliced
- 1 garlic clove, minced
- 2 tablespoons fresh parsley leaves, chopped
- fresh ground pepper
- 1 lime, juice of, small
- 1 (12 ounce) beer (Corona recommended)
- 1 tablespoon Old Bay Seasoning
- 1 1/2-2 lbs shrimp, shelled but tails intact, deveined

Directions

1. Make salsa: Sprinkle salt over tomatoes in colander and toss gently. Let drain 10 minutes.

2. Combine bell pepper, jalapeño, onion, scallions, garlic, parsley, pepper, and lime juice in mixing bowl. Toss gently and stir in drained tomatoes. Let stand at room temperature 30-60 minutes.

3. Prepare shrimp: Heat beer and Old Bay seasoning to boiling in bottom of steamer. Place shrimp in steaming rack and steam, tightly covered, 2 minutes. Stir once, then continue to steam just until shrimp turn pink, 1-2 minutes longer. Transfer shrimp to serving platter.

4. If salsa is too watery, pour off excess liquid. add salsa to shrimp and toss to combine. Serve hot, at room temperature, or chilled.

GARLIC BASIL SHRIMP

Total Time: 10 min   4 Servings
Prep: 5 min   1 Nutrient-Dense Protein Per Serving
Cook: 5 min   1 Whole-Food Fat Per Serving

Ingredients

- 1 1/4 lbs large shrimp, peeled and deveined (20 to 25 per pound)
- 2 tablespoons extra virgin coconut oil
- 3 garlic cloves, minced
- 1/8 teaspoon hot red pepper flakes (or more)

- 3/4 cup dry white wine
- 1/4 cup finely chopped fresh basil leaf
- 1 1/2 cups grape tomatoes, halved
- fresh ground black pepper
- salt

Directions

1. Heat the oil in a large heavy skillet over moderately high heat until hot but not smoking.

2. Add shrimp and sauté, turning over once, until just cooked through, about 2 minutes.

3. Transfer with a slotted spoon to a large bowl.

4. Add garlic and red pepper flakes to the oil remaining in skillet and cook until fragrant, 30 seconds.

5. Add wine and cook over high heat, stirring occasionally, for 3 minutes.

6. Stir in basil and tomatoes and season the sauce with salt and freshly ground black pepper, to taste.

7. Return the shrimp to pan and cook just until heated through.

Garlic Skewered Shrimp

Total Time: 25 min   4 Servings
Prep: 15 min   1 Nutrient-Dense Protein Per Serving
Cook: 10 min   1 Whole-Food Fat Per Serving

Ingredients

- 4 bamboo skewers, roughly 12-inches long
- 1 lb large shrimp, peeled and deveined
- 2 tablespoons reduced sodium soy sauce
- 1 tablespoon extra virgin coconut oil

- 3 garlic cloves, minced
- 1/4 teaspoon red pepper flakes (optional)
- 3 green onions, cut into 1-inch pieces

Directions

1. Prepare grill or preheat broiler.

2. Soak the bamboo skewers in water 20 minutes.

3. Meanwhile, place shrimp in large plastic bag.

4. Combine soy sauce, oil, garlic and red pepper in cup; mix well. Pour into bag containing shrimp. Close bag securely; turn to coat. Marinate at room temperature 15 minutes.

5. Drain shrimp; reserve marinade.

6. Alternatively thread shrimp and onions onto skewers. Place skewers on grid or rack of broiler pan. Brush with reserved marinade; discard any remaining marinade.

7. Grill, covered, over medium-hot coals or broil 5 to 6 inches from heat 5 minutes on each side or until shrimp are pink and opaque.

8. Serve on lettuce-lined plate with lemon wedges.

GINGER SHRIMP AND VEGGIE PACKETS

Total Time: 30 min
Prep: 10 min
Cook: 20 min

4 Servings
1 Non-Starchy Vegetable Per Serving
1 Nutrient-Dense Protein Per Serving
1 Whole-Food Fat Per Serving

Ingredients

- 1 lb medium raw shrimp (peeled and deveined)
- 1 cup sliced mushroom
- 2 cups fresh broccoli florets (frozen would work, but thaw and drain before using)
- 1 small red bell pepper, cut into strips
- 2 cloves garlic, minced
- 1/2 teaspoon grated, minced fresh ginger or 1/2 teaspoon grated, minced fresh ginger
- 1 teaspoon extra virgin coconut oil

Directions

1. Preheat grill to med-high or oven to 450 degrees.

2. Use either foil cooking bags, or pieces of aluminum foil to make a cooking pouch.

3. Add shrimp and vegetables, top with garlic, ginger and oil.

4. To grill: Place foil pouch on grill rack, cook for 15-20 minutes, or until shrimp is no longer pink.

5. To bake in oven: Place pouch in cake pan or cookie sheet with sides.

6. Bake 25-30 minutes, or until shrimp is no longer pink.

JERKED SHRIMP

Total Time: 10 min   4 Servings
Prep: 5 min   1 Nutrient-Dense Protein Per Serving
Cook: 5 min   1 Whole-Food Fat Per Serving

Ingredients

- 1 lb jumbo shrimp
- 1/4 cup butter, melted

- Caribbean jerk seasoning, McCormick

Directions

1. Use 1 pound jumbo shrimp, precooked frozen, peeled and deveined, tails can be either on or off.

2. The most important thing to remember with this recipe is to completely thaw the precooked, frozen shrimp in a colander. When most of the water drains off, pat dry the shrimp as much as possible with paper towels. (Or start with fresh, peeled, deveined shrimp, precooked. A lot of grocers will steam them at no extra charge.).

3. Turn your burner on medium high (almost high) and set your large non stick skillet or wok over the burner. When skillet begins to get really hot, but NOT smoking, quickly add the melted butter and shrimp.

4. Sprinkle on the Caribbean Jerk Seasoning to taste. It's hot and spicy so be careful if you don't like the heat.

5. Keep the shrimp moving in the pan, glazing the shrimp with the hot butter and spices.

6. Cook just until hot and slightly browned. (only about 3 minutes or even less depending on the heat of your skillet).

7. You can also make these in the broiler or on the grill after tossing the shrimp in melted butter, sprinkling on Caribbean Jerk Seasoning and spreading them on a broiler pan or open grill. Broil for only 2 to 3 minutes, watching closely.

Mediterranean Prawns

Total Time: 25 min   4 Servings
Prep: 5 min   1 Nutrient-Dense Protein Per Serving
Cook: 20 min   1 Whole-Food Fat Per Serving

Ingredients

- 2 tablespoons extra virgin coconut oil
- 1 tablespoon minced garlic
- 2 cups chopped fresh or canned tomatoes, drained
- 1/2 cup dry white wine
- 2 tablespoons finely chopped fresh flat-leaf parsley, divided

- 1/2 teaspoon dried marjoram, crushed
- 1/4 teaspoon salt
- 1/4 teaspoon freshly ground black pepper
- 1 1/2 pounds large shrimp, peeled
- 3 ounces feta cheese, cut into 1/2-inch cubes

Directions

1. Heat oil in a large skillet over medium heat. Add garlic; reduce heat to medium-low. Cook until garlic colors, stirring frequently.

2. Add tomatoes, wine, 1 tablespoon parsley, marjoram, salt, and pepper. Cook over medium-high heat until sauce is the thickness of a light purée, stirring occasionally.

3. Add shrimp; cook until shrimp turn pink (about 5 minutes).

4. Add feta, stirring gently (try to keep cheese from crumbling too much).

5. Garnish with remaining parsley.

6. Serve hot.

RED CHILIES SHRIMP

Total Time: 17 min | 4 Servings
Prep: 12 min | 1 Nutrient-Dense Protein Per Serving
Cook: 5 min | 1 Whole-Food Fat Per Serving

Ingredients

- 1 lb shrimp, peeled (medium-sized)
- 5 garlic cloves, diced
- 2 serrano chilies, seeded and minced
- 1/4 cup extra virgin coconut oil
- 1/2 cup sweet rice wine (found in the Asian section of most grocery stores)
- 3 tablespoons tamari (soy sauce)
- 1/4 cup Australian yam-daisy greens, chopped (or fresh scallions)
- 1 meyer lemon, juice of

Directions

1. Sauté the garlic and minced chilies in extra virgin coconut oil over medium-high heat until garlic turns slightly brown.

2. Add the rice wine and cook for 1 minute to evaporate the alcohol.

3. Then add Tamari and lemon aspen (or Meyer lemon) juice.

4. Let cook for 1 minute.

5. Stir, add the shrimp, and raise the heat to high.

6. Cook, stirring often, until the shrimp become pink – between one and two minutes. Then remove from the stove immediately, garnish with chopped scallions, and serve the shrimp, along with the sauce.

Sassy Shrimp

Total Time: 10 min
Prep: 5 min
Cook: 5 min

4 Servings
1 Nutrient-Dense Protein Per Serving
1 Whole-Food Fat Per Serving

Ingredients

- 1 lb small shrimp (peeled & deveined)
- 1/2 teaspoon chives (chopped)
- 2 garlic cloves (chopped)
- 1/4 cup butter

- 1/2 teaspoon salt
- 1 1/2 tablespoons sherry wine
- 1 tablespoon parmesan cheese (grated)

Directions

1. Sauté chives and garlic in butter until tender.

2. Add shrimp and simmer until pink.

3. Add salt and sherry, sprinkle cheese over top.

4. Serve as appetizers or main dish.

SESAME BBQ PRAWNS

Total Time: 28 min
Prep: 20 min
Cook: 8 min

6 Servings
1 Nutrient-Dense Protein Per Serving
1 Whole-Food Fat Per Serving

Ingredients

- 1 kg fresh large green shrimp, 2 lbs (shrimps)
- 1/2 cup soy sauce
- 1/3 cup green onion, chopped
- 1/4 cup extra virgin coconut oil
- 1/4 cup water
- 3 cloves garlic
- 1 1/2 teaspoons ground ginger
- 1/2 teaspoon freshly grated nutmeg

Directions

1. Shell and wash the prawns leaving the tails intact.

2. Combine all ingredients except prawns, mixing well, in a bowl.

3. Add prawns, cover and marinate for 1-2 hours.

4. Remove from marinade.

5. Cook in the BBQ with lid on for 8-15 minutes, or until cooked through (DO NOT OVERCOOK), depending on size.

SHRIMP AND TOMATOES

Total Time: 28 min   4 Servings
Prep: 20 min   1 Nutrient-Dense Protein Per Serving
Cook: 8 min   1 Whole-Food Fat Per Serving

Ingredients

- 7 teaspoons extra virgin coconut oil
- 1 1/2 lbs medium shrimp, peeled, deveined and tails removed
- coarse salt
- pepper
- 3 garlic cloves, thinly sliced

- 1/8 teaspoon dried red pepper flakes
- 6 plum tomatoes, cored, halved lengthwise and sliced 1/2 inch thick
- 2 tablespoons fresh parsley, chopped
- 2 tablespoons fresh lemon juice

Directions

1. In a large nonstick skillet, heat 1 tablespoons extra virgin coconut oil over high heat; swirl to coat pan.

2. Season shrimp with salt and pepper.

3. Add half the shrimp to the pan; cook 3-4 minutes until opaque throughout.

4. Transfer to a plate; repeat with remaining 2 teaspoons of extra virgin coconut oil and shrimp.

5. Reduce heat to medium, add garlic and red pepper flakes; stir in tomatoes; cook 4-6 minutes until they begin to break down.

6. Season with salt.

7. Return shrimp and any accumulate juices to the pan. Add parsley and lemon juice and toss to coat.

SHRIMP BOURBON

Total Time: 1hr   8 Servings
Prep: 30 min   1 Nutrient-Dense Protein Per Serving
Cook: 30 min   1 Whole-Food Fat Per Serving

Ingredients

- 2 lbs medium shrimp (or 2 lbs. of frozen shrimp)
- 2 tablespoons butter
- 2 large shallots, chopped
- 2 garlic cloves, minced
- 3/4 cup chicken broth
- 1/2 cup Bourbon
- 1/2 cup half-and-half
- 1/2 teaspoon ground red pepper
- shredded parmesan cheese (optional)

Directions

1. Peel and devein shrimp.

2. Melt butter in skillet over medium-high heat; add shallots and garlic.

3. Sauté 3 minutes or until tender.

4. Stir in chicken broth, stirring occasionally.

5. Add next 3 ingredients.

6. Stir for 5 minutes or until slightly thickened.

7. Add shrimp; cook 3 minutes or until shrimp turn pink.

8. Remove from heat, and serve with green salad. Sprinkle with Parmesan cheese, if desired.

SHRIMP SCAMPI

Total Time: 10 min   3 Servings
Prep: 5 min   1 Nutrient-Dense Protein Per Serving
Cook: 5 min   1 Whole-Food Fat Per Serving

Ingredients

- 1 tablespoon extra virgin coconut oil
- 1 lb medium shrimp, uncooked deveined peeled
- 1 medium green onion, thinly sliced
- 1/2 teaspoon garlic, minced

- 1/2 teaspoon dried basil leaves
- 3/4 teaspoon parsley flakes
- 1 tablespoon lemon juice
- 1/8 teaspoon salt
- 1 tablespoon parmesan cheese, grated, if desired

Directions

1. Use a 10-inch skillet, with oil heated over medium heat.

2. Add shrimp and all of the remaining ingredients, except parmesan cheese.

3. Cook for 2 to 3 minutes, stirring frequently, until shrimp are just turning pink. Remove from heat.

4. Sprinkle with cheese.

Simplest Shrimp

Total Time: 15 min
Prep: 10 min
Cook: 5 min

4 Servings
1 Nutrient-Dense Protein Per Serving
1 Whole-Food Fat Per Serving

Ingredients

- 1 lb large shrimp (can be shelled, or not shelled, we preferred not)
- 2 tablespoons butter
- 2 tablespoons water (or chicken broth)
- 1 tablespoon Old Bay Seasoning (or any seafood seasoning)

- 1 small onion, sliced very thinly (optional)
- 1 garlic clove, minced fine (optional)
- course ground pepper (optional)
- seafood cocktail sauce, for dipping
- toothpick, for stabbing

Directions

1. Mix together butter, water, (or broth), seasonings, onion, and garlic if using, and pepper, in microwave dish/casserole dish. Heat this fluid/butter for 30/60 seconds on high. Take out carefully, and add shrimp, all in one layer. Add onion and garlic if using.

2. Add extra ingredients if needed/seasonings.

3. Set timer for microwave for 3 minutes, and cook. Make sure to use a plastic wrap to cover dish, venting on one side for air. After 3 minutes, check to make sure the shrimp are cooked through. If not put back into oven for 30 second intervals.

4. Take out shrimp and set on top of crackers, add extra seasonings, and devour.

Sizzling Garlic Prawns

Total Time: 13 min   6 Servings
Prep: 5 min   1 Nutrient-Dense Protein Per Serving
Cook: 8 min   1 Whole-Food Fat Per Serving

Ingredients

- 900 g raw king prawns, peeled and butterflied
- 3 tablespoons parsley, chopped
- 1 teaspoon chili flakes (smoked paprika) or 1-2 teaspoon pimentos (smoked paprika)

- 4 tablespoons extra virgin coconut oil
- 4-6 garlic cloves, thinly sliced
- 4-6 tablespoons dry sherry

Directions

1. Heat the oven to 220C/fan 200C/gas 7.

2. Preparing prawns: To butterfly the prawns simply slit the prawns lengthways but don't go all the way through and remove the vein.

3. Divide the prawns, garlic, chilli or pimenton, sherry and olive oil between 6 small ovenproof dishes or use 1 large one.

4. Cook for 8 – 12 minutes, depending on the size of the dish or dishes, or until pink and sizzling.

5. Sprinkle with the parsley and serve with lemon wedges.

SPANISH GARLIC SHRIMP

Total Time: 15 min
Prep: 10 min
Cook: 5 min

4 Servings
1 Nutrient-Dense Protein Per Serving
1 Whole-Food Fat Per Serving

Ingredients

- 1/4 cup extra virgin coconut oil
- 4 large garlic cloves, finely minced
- 1 teaspoon red pepper flakes
- 1 lb medium shrimp, peeled and deveined
- 2 tablespoons fresh lemon juice
- 2 tablespoons dry sherry
- 1 teaspoon paprika
- chopped fresh flat-leaf parsley (to garnish, Italian)

Directions

1. In a sauté pan over medium heat, warm the extra virgin coconut oil.

2. Add the garlic and red pepper flakes and sauté for 1 minute.

3. Raise the heat to high and add the shrimp, lemon juice, sherry and paprika. Stir well, then sauté, stirring briskly, until the shrimp turn pink and curl slightly, about 3 minutes.

4. Season to taste with salt and freshly ground black pepper and sprinkle with parsley. Serve hot.

Spanish Shrimp in Garlic

Total Time: 16 min   4 Servings
Prep: 10 min   1 Nutrient-Dense Protein Per Serving
Cook: 6 min   1 Whole-Food Fat Per Serving

Ingredients

- 1/3 cup extra virgin coconut oil
- 4 garlic cloves, chopped
- 2 bay leaves

- 1 teaspoon Tabasco sauce
- 1 lb medium raw shrimp, cleaned
- salt, to taste

Directions

1. In large skillet heat 1/3 cup extra virgin coconut oil; stir in 4 cloves garlic, chopped, 2 bay leaves, and 1 teaspoon Tabasco pepper sauce.

2. When garlic sizzles, add 1 pound medium-sized, raw, cleaned shrimp.

3. Stir-fry until shrimp are pink (about 3 minutes).

4. Sprinkle with salt to taste.

Tilapia

Caper and White Tilapia

Total Time: 20 min
Prep: 5 min
Cook: 15 min

2 Servings
1 Nutrient-Dense Protein Per Serving
1 Whole-Food Fat Per Serving

Ingredients

- 1 teaspoon fennel seed (toast briefly and set aside)
- 12 ounces tilapia fillets
- 1 tablespoon Dijon mustard
- 1/8 teaspoon salt

- 1/8 teaspoon fresh ground black pepper
- 2 tablespoons capers (drained well)
- 1/4 cup dry white wine

Directions

1. Preheat oven to 425 degrees.

2. In a medium-hot iron skillet briefly toast fennel seeds.

3. In a large Pyrex baking dish sprayed with cooking spray, arrange fillets in a single layer.

4. Spread mustard on the fillets, and sprinkle with salt and pepper.

5. Top with capers and fennel seeds.

6. Pour wine around fish. Oven-roast uncovered for 15-17 minutes, or until cooked through, and some of the wine has evaporated.

CILANTRO TILAPIA

Total Time: 17 min
Prep: 5 min
Cook: 12 min

4 Servings
1 Nutrient-Dense Protein Per Serving
1 Whole-Food Fat Per Serving

Ingredients

- 3 tablespoons extra virgin coconut oil
- 4 (4 ounce) tilapia fillets, fresh
- 2 tablespoons garlic salt

- 2 tablespoons cajun seasoning
- black pepper, to taste
- 1 bunch cilantro

Directions

1. Preheat oven to 375.

2. Coat the bottom of a baking dish with extra virgin coconut oil.

3. Place the tilapia fillets in the pan.

4. Sprinkle desired amount of garlic salt, cajun seasoning, and pepper over tilapia pieces.

5. Press several sprigs of cilantro on top of each piece.

6. Bake tilapia for 8 to 12 minutes.

7. Enjoy alone or with lemon!

TILAPIA PARMESAN

Total Time: 20 min   8 Servings
Prep: 10 min   1 Nutrient-Dense Protein Per Serving
Cook: 10 min   1 Whole-Food Fat Per Serving

Ingredients

- 1-1/2 cups grated Parmesan cheese
- 1 tablespoon and 1 teaspoon paprika
- 2 tablespoons chopped fresh parsley

- salt and ground black pepper to taste
- 8 tilapia fillets
- extra virgin coconut oil

Directions

1. Preheat oven to 400 degrees F (200 degrees C). Line a baking sheet with aluminum foil.

2. Whisk Parmesan cheese, paprika, parsley, salt, and pepper together in a shallow dish.

3. Coat tilapia fillets with melted extra virgin coconut oil and press into the Parmesan cheese mixture. Arrange coated fillets on the prepared baking sheet.

4. Bake in preheated oven until the fish flakes easily with a fork, 10 to 12 minutes.

TILAPIA PARMESAN

Total Time: 20 min
Prep: 10 min
Cook: 10 min

4 Servings
1 Nutrient-Dense Protein Per Serving
1 Whole-Food Fat Per Serving

Ingredients

- 4 (3 ounce) tilapia fillets
- 3/4 cup freshly grated parmesan cheese
- 1 teaspoon chopped flat leaf parsley
- 1 teaspoon dried rosemary

- 2 teaspoons paprika
- 1 lemon, cut into wedges
- 1/4 cup extra virgin coconut oil, for drizzling
- salt
- fresh ground pepper

Directions

1. Preheat the oven to 400 degrees.

2. In a shallow dish, combine the cheese with the paprika and parsley and season with salt and pepper.

3. Drizzle the fish with extra virgin coconut oil and dredge in the cheese mixture.

4. Place on a foil lined baking sheet and bake until the fish is opaque in the thickest part, 10 to 12 minutes.

5. Serve the fish with the lemon wedges.

Tomato Lemon Fish Bake

Total Time: 12 min
Prep: 2 min
Cook: 10 min

3 Servings
1 Nutrient-Dense Protein Per Serving
1 Whole-Food Fat Per Serving

Ingredients

- 3/4-1 lb fresh tilapia fillets or 3/4-1 lb other white fish fillet
- 1 lemon
- 1 tomato

- 1/4 teaspoon dried thyme or 3/4 teaspoon fresh thyme
- 2 tablespoons white wine (optional)

Directions

1. Preheat oven to 500 degrees.

2. Slice lemon and tomato into thin slices.

3. Lay fillets in a single layer in a baking dish.

4. Bake for 3 to 5 minutes, until they start to draw up and turn white.

5. Remove from oven.

6. Alternate slices of lemon and tomato on fish.

7. Sprinkle with thyme and wine (if using).

8. Bake 3 to 5 minutes more, or longer, until fish flakes with a fork.

TUNA

MELT IN YOUR MOUTH TUNA STEAKS

Total Time: 30 min
Prep: 20 min
Cook: 10 min

8 Servings
1 Nutrient-Dense Protein Per Serving
2 Whole-Food Fats Per Serving

Ingredients

- 2 pounds fresh tuna steaks
- 1/2 cup soy sauce
- 1/2 cup sherry
- 1/2 cup extra virgin coconut oil
- 1 bunch green onions, finely chopped
- 1/2 cup minced fresh ginger root
- 3 cloves garlic, minced
- 1 teaspoon salt
- 1 teaspoon ground black pepper

Directions

1. Place tuna steaks in a steamer over 1 inch of boiling water, and cover. Cook 6 to 8 minutes, or until fish flakes easily with a fork.

2. Meanwhile, in a medium saucepan, combine soy sauce, sherry, extra virgin coconut oil, green onions, ginger, garlic, salt, and black pepper. Bring to a boil.

3. Remove tuna steaks from steamer, and place in a serving dish. Pour sauce over tuna steaks, and serve immediately.

Tuna Teriyaki

Total Time: 25 min
Prep: 15 min
Cook: 10 min

8 Servings
1 Nutrient-Dense Protein Per Serving
1 Whole-Food Fat Per Serving

Ingredients

- 2 cups teriyaki sauce
- 1-1/2 cups extra virgin coconut oil
- 1/4 cup minced garlic

- 2 teaspoons ground black pepper
- 8 (4 ounce) fillets yellowfin tuna

Directions

1. In a large resealable plastic bag, combine the teriyaki sauce, melted oil, garlic, and pepper. Place the tuna fillets in the bag. Seal the bag with as little air in it as possible. Give the mix a good shake, to ensure the tuna fillets are well coated. Marinate for 30 minutes in the refrigerator.

2. Meanwhile, preheat an outdoor grill for high heat, and lightly oil grate.

3. Remove tuna from marinade, and place on grill. For rare tuna, grill for 3 to 5 minutes on each side. For medium, grill 5 to 8 minutes per side. For well done, grill for 8 to 10 minutes per side.

OTHER FISH & SEAFOOD

AVOCADO MAHI MAHI

Total Time: 27 min
Prep: 15 min
Cook: 12 min

6 Servings
1 Nutrient-Dense Protein Per Serving
1 Whole-Food Fat Per Serving

Ingredients

- SALSA
- 1 ripe avocado
- 2 roma tomatoes
- 1 cup minced red onion
- 1 jalapeno pepper, minced
- 1/2 cup fresh cilantro
- 1 lime, juice of
- 1/2 teaspoon kosher salt

- MAHI MAHI
- 3 lbs mahi mahi, cut into 6 pieces
- 1 tablespoon extra virgin coconut oil
- 1 lime, juice of
- 1/2 teaspoon kosher salt

Directions

1. Cut avocado, tomato into 1/2 inch chunks, add minced onion, and jalapeno, cilantro and lime juice and salt.

2. Mix together and store in fridge can be made hours before.

3. Meanwhile take mahi mahi and cut into strips.

4. Add extra virgin coconut oil, lime, salt and pepper and marinate for 20-30 minutes.

5. Grill over coals or on a grill or under broiler for 6-8 minutes per side.

6. Serve fish with salsa on top.

BLACKENED FISH

Total Time: 10 min   4 Servings
Prep: 5 min   1 Nutrient-Dense Protein Per Serving
Cook: 5 min   1 Whole-Food Fat Per Serving

Ingredients

- 4 red snapper fillets or 4 other firm fish (about 1 1/2 pounds raw fish)
- 1 teaspoon salt
- 1 tablespoon garlic powder
- 2 teaspoons dried thyme
- 1 tablespoon dried parsley flakes

- 1 tablespoon dried basil
- 1-2 teaspoon cayenne pepper (depending on how hot you want it)
- 1/4 teaspoon fresh ground black pepper
- 1 tablespoon extra virgin coconut oil

Directions

1. Combine all spices/dry ingredients in a bowl and mix well.

2. Spread the spice mixture onto a flat plate.

3. Press the fish fillets firmly into the spices, coating both sides.

4. Heat the extra virgin coconut oil until almost smoking in a large heavy skillet.

5. Cook the fish about 2 1/2 minutes on each side for fillets less than 3/4 inch thick.

6. Increase time slightly for thicker fillets.

Cajun Catfish

Total Time: 20 min   4 Servings
Prep: 10 min   1 Nutrient-Dense Protein Per Serving
Cook: 10 min   1 Whole-Food Fat Per Serving

Ingredients

- 2 tablespoons extra virgin coconut oil
- 1 tablespoon paprika
- 1 teaspoon dried oregano
- 1/2 teaspoon salt
- 1/4 teaspoon cayenne
- 4 catfish fillets (about 1 1/2 pounds)

Directions

1. Preheat broiler.

2. Line pan with foil for easy clean up.

3. Combine oil, paprika, oregano, salt and cayenne pepper in a small bowl.

4. Place catfish on foil-lined pan and brush both sides with spice mixture. Arrange catfish, flat side up, for initial cooking.

5. Broil about 10 minutes (until catfish reaches an internal temperature of 145 degrees F), carefully turning fillets once halfway through cooking. Don't overcook!

Cheddar Pollock

Total Time: 40 min
Prep: 15 min
Cook: 25 min

4 Servings
2 Nutrient-Dense Protein Per Serving
2 Whole-Food Fats Per Serving
1 Most-Dairy Per Serving

Ingredients

- 8 (6 ounce) fillets pollock fillets
- 2 teaspoons paprika
- 2 teaspoons black pepper
- 4 small yellow onion, sliced
- 4 small green bell pepper, cut into strips
- 16 (1/4 inch thick) slices red tomato
- 16 slices Cheddar cheese

Directions

1. Preheat oven to 350 degrees F (175 degrees C). Spray a baking sheet with butter flavored cooking spray.

2. Season the pollock fillets with paprika and black pepper. Place on baking sheet and layer with onion, green pepper, and tomato slices.

3. Bake in preheated oven until fish has cooked and flakes easily, about 15 minutes. Turn oven off, place two slices of cheese on each fillet. Return fish to the oven and allow cheese to melt, about 3 minutes.

Chilean Fish Bake

Total Time: 25 min   6 Servings
Prep: 15 min   1 Nutrient-Dense Protein Per Serving
Cook: 10 min   1 Whole-Food Fat Per Serving

Ingredients

- 1 3/4 lbs sea bass fillets, cut into 6 pieces
- 2 tangerines (zest and juice one, peel and segment the other)
- 4 scallions, chopped
- 1 garlic clove, peeled and chopped
- 2 tablespoons unsalted butter, cubed
- pepper, to taste

Directions

1. Heat oven to 450°F

2. Place Chilean sea bass fillet, cut into 6 pieces, into greased 9 x13 glass dish.

3. From the two tangerines, zest and juice 1; peel and segment the other one.

4. Top the fillets with the tangerine segments, chopped scallions, and garlic.

5. Pour 1/3 cup tangerine juice and 1 tsp zest over fish.

6. Dot with 2 tbsp unsalted butter, cubed.

7. Cook 10 minutes or until fish flakes easily with a fork.

8. Add pepper to taste and enjoy.

Cook Microwave Fish

Total Time: 22 min   4 Servings
Prep: 15 min   1 Nutrient-Dense Protein Per Serving
Cook: 7 min   1 Whole-Food Fat Per Serving

Ingredients

- 1 lb fresh fish fillets or 1 lb frozen fish fillet
- 1/3 cup chopped cucumber
- 2 tablespoons reduced-calorie mayonnaise
- 2 tablespoons plain low-fat yogurt
- 1 1/2 teaspoons prepared mustard

Directions

1. Thaw fish, if frozen.

2. Turn under any thin edges of fish.

3. In a 12 x 7½ x 2-inch baking dish (use an 8x8x2-inch baking dish for low-wattage ovens) arrange fish fillets with thicker portions toward outer edges of the dish.

4. Cover dish with vented clear plastic wrap.

5. Cook on 100% power (high) for 4 to 7 minutes or till fish flakes easily when tested with a fork, giving dish a half-turn after 3 minutes.

6. Meanwhile, for sauce, in a small bowl stir together cucumber, mayonnaise, yogurt, and mustard.

7. Serve with fish.

Cost-Effective Lobster

Total Time: 25 min   2 Servings
Prep: 5 min   1 Nutrient-Dense Protein Per Serving
Cook: 20 min   1 Whole-Food Fat Per Serving

Ingredients

- 1 lb frozen haddock
- 2 cups water
- 1 tablespoon vinegar
- 1 teaspoon Old Bay Seasoning or 1 teaspoon lemon pepper
- melted butter

Directions

1. Combine first four ingredients put in a large sauce pan.

2. Bring to a boil.

3. Reduce heat and simmer for 20 minutes.

4. Drain liquid.

5. Serve with melted butter.

CRISPY SMELTS

Total Time: 20 min
Prep: 10 min
Cook: 10 min

6 Servings
1 Nutrient-Dense Protein Per Serving
1 Whole-Food Fat Per Serving

Ingredients

- 2 1/4 lbs smelt (fresh)
- 1 1/2 teaspoons salt
- coconut flour
- 3 tablespoons butter

Directions

1. Clean fish, and remove the heads.

2. Rinse fish well, and drain.

3. Salt the fish, lightly coat in the coconut flour, then fry in the butter until golden brown on both sides.

4. Serve immediately.

Fancy Fish in Foil

Total Time: 20 min   2 Servings
Prep: 5 min   1 Nutrient-Dense Protein Per Serving
Cook: 15 min   1 Whole-Food Fat Per Serving

Ingredients

- 1 lb white fish fillet
- 1 lime, sliced
- 1 small onion, sliced thin
- 1 teaspoon extra virgin coconut oil

- 1 teaspoon oregano
- 1 dash cumin
- 1 garlic clove, minced
- 2 tablespoons fresh cilantro, chopped

Directions

1. Place fish in the middle of a double layer of heavy foil.

2. Drizzle with oil and sprinkle with all other seasonings.

3. Fold up foil edges and seal well.

4. Place on grill (hot coals) or broil for 15-20 minutes.

FIERY HALIBUT

Total Time: 20 min
Prep: 5 min
Cook: 15 min

4 Servings
1 Nutrient-Dense Protein Per Serving
1 Whole-Food Fat Per Serving

Ingredients

- 4 (4 -6 ounce) alaska halibut steaks, fresh, thawed, frozen
- 1 tablespoon paprika
- 1 1/2 teaspoons dried oregano
- 1 1/2 teaspoons dried thyme
- 1 teaspoon onion powder

- 1 teaspoon garlic powder
- 1 teaspoon black pepper
- 1 teaspoon salt
- 1/2 teaspoon cayenne pepper
- 1 1/2 tablespoons butter, melted

Directions

1. Preheat broiler/oven or grill to medium-high heat.

2. Mix together all dry seasoning ingredients until well combined.

3. Rinse any ice glaze from frozen Alaska Halibut under cold water, pat dry with paper towel. Place halibut on a spray-coated or foil-lined baking sheet. Brush butter onto top surfaces of halibut and sprinkle with 1/2 teaspoon seasoning mixture (note: for best results with frozen fish, cook halibut 4 minutes before adding butter and spices.).

4. Grill or broil halibut 5-7 inches from heat for 13 minutes for frozen halibut OR 8 minutes for fresh/thawed fish. Cook just until fish is opaque throughout.

5. Store remaining seasoning mixture in an airtight container for future use.

FISH TACOS

Total Time: 1hr   8 Servings
Prep: 30 min   1 Nutrient-Dense Protein Per Serving
Cook: 30 min   1 Whole-Food Fat Per Serving

Ingredients

- 2 tablespoons finely diced white onions
- 2 tablespoons extra virgin coconut oil
- 2 tablespoons freshly squeezed lime juice
- 2 tablespoons freshly squeezed orange juice
- 1 tablespoon fresh lemon juice
- 1 tablespoon chopped cilantro
- 1 teaspoon minced garlic

- 1/2 teaspoon dried oregano, rubbed to a powder
- 1/4 teaspoon kosher salt
- 1 1/2 lbs boneless skinless white fish fillets
- corn tortilla, warmed
- diced avocados or smashed avocado, with
- lime juice, and
- salt
- lime wedge
- mango salsa (Mango Salsa)
- salsa

Directions

1. Combine all marinade ingredients. Cut the fish into several large pieces and add to the marinade.

2. Refrigerate for 1 to 3 hours (no longer or you'll have ceviche). Drain the fish and discard the marinade.

3. Half an hour before cooking, clean the grill thoroughly with a brush and wipe it down with an oil-dampened rag. Preheat the grill on high. Grill the fish until it is barely firm to the touch and opaque through the center. Do not overcook.

4. Remove to a platter and break into chunks to serve. Keep loosely covered.

5. To serve, hold a tortilla in your hand and add a spoonful of avocado. Add a few pieces of fish, a squeeze of lime, mango salsa; finish with the optional toppings.

6. Note: The fish may also be baked or sautéed.

GARLIC SCALLOPS

Total Time: 22 min
Prep: 10 min
Cook: 12 min

6 Servings
1 Nutrient-Dense Protein Per Serving
1 Whole-Food Fat Per Serving

Ingredients

- 12 scallops
- 2 garlic cloves, smashed
- 4 ounces butter

- 3 tablespoons chopped parsley
- salt and black pepper

Directions

1. Wash and dry the scallops and separate the coral from the white flesh.

2. Peel and smash the garlic.

3. Melt half the butter in a saucepan and cook the white flesh very gently for 10 minutes, until tender.

4. Season to taste.

5. Place on paper towel and keep hot between two plates over a pan of hot water.

6. Pour out the butter from the pan, wipe it out with paper and add the remaining butter and the coral, cook for 1 minute only on each side.

7. Add the white flesh and the herbs and garlic, leave over the heat just long enough to mix thoroughly and divide between the heated shells, (plates).

8. Serve immediately with a dry rose wine.

GRILLED SWORDFISH

Total Time: 22 min
Prep: 10 min
Cook: 12 min

8 Servings
2 Nutrient-Dense Protein Per Serving
2 Whole-Food Fats Per Serving

Ingredients

- 8 (8 ounce) swordfish steaks
- 1 cup teriyaki sauce

- 1/4 cup margarine, softened
- 2 teaspoons garlic powder

Directions

1. Preheat outdoor grill for medium heat.

2. Marinate swordfish in teriyaki sauce for 5 minutes per side.

3. Lightly oil grill grate. Grill steaks, basting frequently with melted margarine, for 5 to 6 minutes per side, or until fish flakes easily with a fork. Season with garlic powder, and serve.

HERBED LIME FISH

Total Time: 35 min
Prep: 10 min
Cook: 25 min

4 Servings
1 Nutrient-Dense Protein Per Serving
1 Whole-Food Fat Per Serving

Ingredients

- 4 cod fish fillets (firm fish fillets) or 4 red snapper fillets (firm fish fillets)
- 1/4 cup lime juice
- 4 garlic cloves, minced
- 1/2 cup chopped fresh parsley
- 1/2 cup chopped scallion
- 1/2 teaspoon dried rosemary
- 1/2 teaspoon dried thyme
- 1 teaspoon sweet paprika
- 1 cup diced fresh tomato

Directions

1. Preheat oven to 375.

2. In a medium bowl, mix the lime juice, garlic, parsley, scallions, rosemary, thyme, paprika and tomatoes. Place the fillets in an unoiled baking dish and spread the topping over the fish.

3. Cover tightly with foil and bake for about 25 minutes, until the fish flakes easily with a fork.

Italian Basa

Total Time: 16 min
Prep: 10 min
Cook: 6 min

2 Servings
1 Nutrient-Dense Protein Per Serving
1 Whole-Food Fat Per Serving

Ingredients

- 14 ounces basa fillets
- 2 tablespoons fresh lemon juice
- 1 teaspoon dried oregano

- 1/2 teaspoon fresh coarse ground black pepper
- 1 jalapeno pepper, chopped fine
- 2 roma tomatoes, chopped

Directions

1. If using frozen fish nake sure it is fully thawed and patted dry of any moisture.

2. Drizzle half the lemon juice on one side of the filet, sprinkle on the pepper & oregano, then pat them on the fish.

3. Turn the filet over and repeat with the lemon & spices.

4. Turn you heat to medium, heat a large skillet & lightly spray with oil or Pam.

5. Add the fish, tomatoes & Jalapeno, cover.

6. Cook for 3 minutes, flip the fish and stir the tomatoe, cover.

7. Finish cooking apprx 3 more minutes.

8. Simple & easy serve with rice or noodles.

LEMON AND CAPERS CATFISH

Total Time: 18 min   8 Servings
Prep: 13 min   1 Nutrient-Dense Protein Per Serving
Cook: 5 min   1 Whole-Food Fat Per Serving

Ingredients

- 4 (1/4 lb) skinless catfish fillet
- 1/2 teaspoon black pepper
- 1 grated small lemon, juice and zest of
- 2 tablespoons orange juice
- 2 teaspoons capers, rinsed
- 1 teaspoon extra virgin coconut oil
- 1 tablespoon chopped fresh oregano
- 1/2 seedless cucumber, thinly sliced

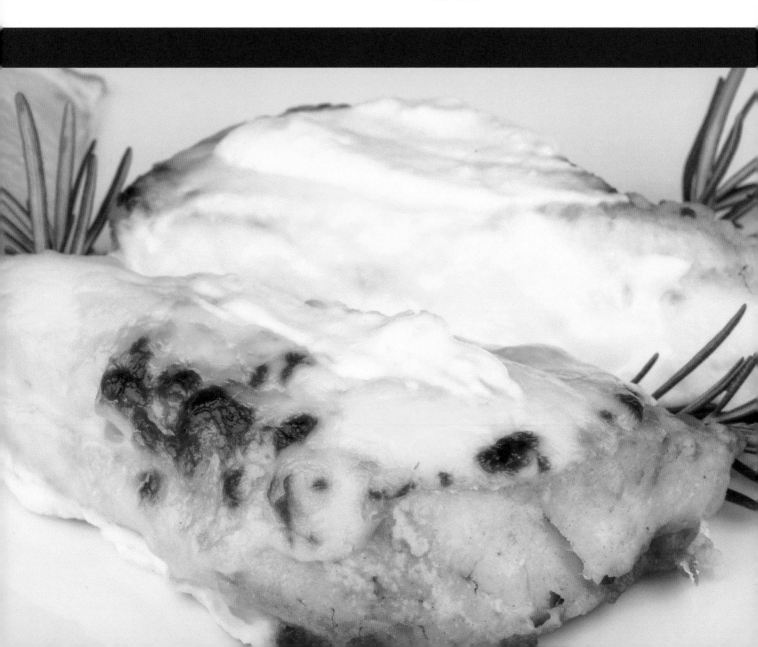

Directions

1. Spray the rack of a broiler pan with nonstick spray; preheat broiler.

2. Put the catfish on the prepared rack. Lightly spray the fish with nonstick spray and sprinkle with 1/4 teaspoon black pepper. Broil the fish 5 inches from the heat just until opaque in the center, about 8 minutes. (Tip: To check if the fish is cooked properly, slit the thickest part of fish fillets with a thin-bladed knife. Peek inside; the flesh should be opaque and should flake easily.).

3. Meanwhile, whisk the lemon zest and juice, orange juice, capers, oil, oregano, and the remaining 1/4 teaspoon pepper in a small bowl.

4. Divide the cucumbers among 4 plates. Top each serving with 1 fillet; drizzle evenly with the dressing.

MACKEREL WITH LEMON AND GARLIC

Total Time: 15 min
Prep: 10 min
Cook: 5 min

4 Servings
1 Nutrient-Dense Protein Per Serving
1 Whole-Food Fat Per Serving

Ingredients

- 4 (100 g) mackerel fillets
- 2 garlic cloves, minced
- 1/2 lemon, juice of
- salt
- pepper

Directions

1. Lay the fillets of fish on a baking tray, which has been covered with foil for easy clean up.

2. Sprinkle with salt and leave for 5-10 minutes. This helps give the flesh a firmer texture but you may omit this step if you prefer.

3. Meanwhile, preheat the oven grill.

4. Mix together the garlic, lemon and some freshly ground black pepper.

5. Pour over the mackerel and then put in the oven to grill for about 5 minutes.

6. If you have some fresh herbs like parsley to hand you could finely chop them and sprinkle them over the fish at this point.

7. Serve with your favourite veggies.

Mediterranean Orange Roughy

Total Time: 25 min   4 Servings
Prep: 10 min   1 Nutrient-Dense Protein Per Serving
Cook: 15 min   1 Whole-Food Fat Per Serving

Ingredients

- 1 garlic clove, finely chopped
- 1-2 tablespoon extra virgin coconut oil
- 4 (4 -6 ounce) fish fillets
- 2 cups roasted red peppers, chopped (preroasted, storebought is fine)
- 1/2 onion, chopped
- 1/2 cup black olives (preferably halfed or sliced)
- 1 pinch salt or 1 pinch pepper, to taste

Directions

1. Preheat your oven to 400 degrees F.

2. Heat the extra virgin coconut oil in a nonstick skillet and sauté the garlic for a min or so.

3. Add the onions, cook about halfway to done. Turn off the stove.

4. Add the roasted red peppers last, they're already cooked so only need to be heated through for a min or so.

5. Place each raw fillet in their own aluminum foil pack or 2 fillets per 1 pack if you want to save foil.

6. Spoon the onion/pepper/garlic mixture made above over the fillets and then the olives too.

7. Close the foil around the fish, leaving a teeny hole for steam escape.

8. Bake for about 15-20 minutes, fish should flake easily with a fork.

MEDITERRANEAN STUFFED SWORDFISH

Total Time: 30 min
Prep: 15 min
Cook: 15 min

2 Servings
1 Non-Starchy Vegetable Per Serving
1 Nutrient-Dense Protein Per Serving
1 Whole-Food Fat Per Serving

Ingredients

- 1 (8-10 ounce) swordfish steaks (about 2-inch thick)
- 1 tablespoon fresh lemon juice
- 2 cups fresh spinach
- 4 teaspoons extra virgin coconut oil
- 1 garlic clove, minced
- 1/4 cup crumbled feta

Directions

1. Preheat an outdoor grill for high heat and lightly oil grate.

2. Cut a slit in steak to create a pocket that is open on side only. In a cup. mix together 1 tablespoon extra virgin coconut oil and lemon juice; brush over both sides of fish. Set aside.

3. In a small skillet, heat 1 teaspoon extra virgin coconut oil and garlic over medium heat. Cook spinach in oil until just wilted. Remove from heat, and stuff into pocket. Place feta in pocket over spinach.

4. Arrange fish on grill and cook 5-6 minutes. Turn over and continue cooking until cooked through. Do not over cook.

MUSTARD FISH

Total Time: 45 min   2 Servings
Prep: 30 min   1 Nutrient-Dense Protein Per Serving
Cook: 15 min   1 Whole-Food Fat Per Serving

Ingredients

- 1 1/2 lbs cod or scrod fish or haddock or other firm white fish fillets
- 1/4 cup smooth or coarse Dijon mustard
- 1/3 cup fresh lemon juice
- 1/2 teaspoon dried thyme

- 1-2 teaspoon prepared horseradish
- 2 teaspoons lemon zest, grated
- 1/4 teaspoon ground black pepper

Directions

1. Rinse and dry the fish fillets and place them, skin side down, in a lightly oiled baking pan.

2. Whisk the marinade ingredients together in a mixing bowl or whirl them in a blender or small food processor.

3. Pour the marinade over the fish, turning the fillets to coat both sides.

4. Set aside in the refrigerator for 20 to 60 minutes.

5. Preheat the oven to 400.

6. Place the baking dish, uncovered, in the oven and bake for 10 to 15 minutes, or until the fish is tender and flakes easily with a fork.

MUSTARD SNAPPER

Total Time: 17 min
Prep: 5 min
Cook: 12 min

4 Servings
1 Nutrient-Dense Protein Per Serving
1 Whole-Food Fat Per Serving

Ingredients

- 4 (6 ounce) red snapper fillets
- 3 tablespoons lemon juice
- 2 tablespoons French's Dijon Mustard
- 2 tablespoons mayonnaise
- 2 stalks green onions, finely chopped
- salt and pepper, to taste

Directions

1. Arrange fish fillets in a baking pan or baking dish.

2. Sprinkle fish with lemon juice, salt and pepper.

3. Broil fish in oven for about 7 to 9 minutes or until fish is opaque.

4. Meanwhile, mix prepared mustard, mayonnaise, green onions and salt.

5. Spread sauce over fish and broil for a couple more minutes or until sauce begin to bubble.

6. Serve immediately.

Pecan Cajun Catfish

Total Time: 50 min   6 Servings
Prep: 30 min   1 Nutrient-Dense Protein Per Serving
Cook: 20 min   1 Whole-Food Fat Per Serving
    1 Most-Dairy Per Serving

Ingredients

- 1 lb catfish fillet
- 1 tablespoon lemon juice
- 2 tablespoons extra virgin coconut oil
- 1 tablespoon cajun seasoning (Tony Chachere's)

- 1 teaspoon thyme
- 1/3 cup pecans, chopped
- 2 tablespoons parmesan cheese, grated
- 1 tablespoon parsley, chopped

Directions

1. Preheat oven to 425 degrees.

2. Coat a shallow baking dish with nonstick cooking spray.

3. Place fish in pan and set aside.

4. Combine oil, cajun seasoning, lemon juice and thyme in a small bowl and mix well.

5. Spoon or brush half of the mixture on the fish.

6. Combine chopped pecans, parsley, parmesan cheese and the remaining half of the oil mixture in a small bowl and mix well.

7. Spread mixture onto fish filets.

8. Bake for 10 to 15 minutes (longer depending on the thickness of the fish) or until fish flakes easily. Garnish with parsley sprigs and lemon wedges.

Pistachio Mahi

Total Time: 27 min
Prep: 5 min
Cook: 22 min

6 Servings
1 Nutrient-Dense Protein Per Serving
1 Whole-Food Fat Per Serving

Ingredients

- 6 (5 ounce) fresh mahi mahi fillets
- 5 tablespoons lemon juice
- 1/4 teaspoon black pepper

- 1/2 cup pistachio nut, coarsely chopped
- 2 tablespoons butter, melted
- 1 dash salt

Directions

1. Preheat the oven to 350°F.

2. Place the fillets on a baking sheet and season with the lemon juice, pepper, and salt if desired.

3. Top with the pistachio nuts and drizzle with the melted butter.

4. Bake for 20 to 22 minutes or until the fish flakes easily with a fork; serve immediately.

SALSA FISH FILLETS

Total Time: 12 min
Prep: 2 min
Cook: 10 min

3 Servings
1 Nutrient-Dense Protein Per Serving
1 Whole-Food Fat Per Serving

Ingredients

- 1 (10 ounce) package fish fillets, thawed
- 1/2 cup salsa

- 2 tablespoons parmesan cheese, grated (or more, to taste)

Directions

1. Preheat oven to 425°F.

2. Place thawed fish fillets in a 9 inch pie plate.

3. Spread with salsa and top with Parmesan.

4. Bake, uncovered, until bubbling (about 8 to 12 min).

SEAFOOD BAKE

Total Time: 20 min   8 Servings
Prep: 10 min   2 Nutrient-Dense Protein Per Serving
Cook: 10 min   1 Whole-Food Fat Per Serving

Ingredients

- 8 (4 ounce) halibut fillets
- 24 scallops
- 24 peeled and deveined jumbo shrimp, tail still attached
- 1-1/3 cups dry white wine
- 1/2 cup melted butter

- 1/4 cup lemon juice
- 2 teaspoons seafood seasoning, such as Old Bay™
- 1 tablespoon and 1 teaspoon minced garlic
- Salt and pepper to taste
- 1/4 cup chopped fresh parsley

Directions

1. Preheat oven to 450 degrees F (230 degrees C).

2. Arrange the halibut, scallops, and shrimp in an oven-safe, glass baking dish. Drizzle with wine, butter, and lemon juice. Sprinkle with the seasoning and garlic. Season to taste with salt and pepper.

3. Bake in preheated oven until the halibut has turned white, and is flaky, 10 to 12 minutes. Sprinkle with parsley just before serving.

Seared Sea Scallops

Total Time: 5 min   4 Servings
Prep: 1 min   1 Nutrient-Dense Protein Per Serving
Cook: 4 min   1 Whole-Food Fat Per Serving

Ingredients

- 1 lb sea scallops, rinsed and pat dry
- salt and pepper
- 1 tablespoon extra virgin coconut oil
- 1 tablespoon butter

Directions

1. Heat the extra virgin coconut oil and butter in a large pan over medium-high heat.

2. Salt and pepper both sides of the scallops and place them in the pan. Whatever you do, do not move the scallops at all until ready to flip.

3. Sear the scallops on each side for 1.5 minutes, then remove from the pan and serve.

SIMPLE SEARED SCALLOPS

Total Time: 11 min
Prep: 5 min
Cook: 6 min

2 Servings
1 Nutrient-Dense Protein Per Serving
1 Whole-Food Fat Per Serving

Ingredients

- 1/2 lb fresh sea scallop
- 1 tablespoon extra virgin coconut oil

- 2 tablespoons chopped chives
- salt & freshly ground black pepper

Directions

1. Rinse scallops in cool water, drain and set aside.

2. Heat oil in non-stick skillet. When smoking, add scallops and sauté on high 3 minutes, turning after 1 minute.

3. Add salt and pepper to taste.

4. Sprinkle chives over scallops.

Simple Steamed Veggies and Sole

Total Time: 45 min
Prep: 30 min
Cook: 15 min

4 Servings
1 Non-Starchy Vegetable Per Serving
1 Nutrient-Dense Protein Per Serving
1 Whole-Food Fat Per Serving

Ingredients

- 4 tablespoons light soy sauce, divided
- 3 tablespoons dry white wine
- 1 teaspoon onion powder
- 1/2 teaspoon sugar
- 1 1/2 teaspoons minced fresh gingerroot

- 4 fresh sole fillets, each about 4 ounces
- 1 large carrot, julienned
- 1 medium zucchini, julienned
- 3 tablespoons minced green onions, and tops divided

Directions

1. Combine 3 tablespoons soy sauce, wine, onion powder, sugar and ginger in shallow pan; add fillets, turning to coat both sides well. Let stand 10 minutes; turn over once.

2. Meanwhile, toss carrot and zucchini with remaining soy sauce; pour off excess sauce. Turn vegetables out onto 8-inch round heatproof plate.

3. Remove fillets from marinade; spread out flat and sprinkle with 2 tablespoons green onions. Starting at thinner end, roll up fillet, jellyroll fashion; arrange, seam side down, on vegetables.

4. Place plate on large steamer rack set in large pot or wok of boiling water. (Do not allow water level to reach plate.) Steam, covered, 12 minutes, or until fish flakes easily with fork.

5. Sprinkle remaining 1 tablespoons green onions evenly over fish.

SOLE FLORENTINE

Total Time: 40 min
Prep: 15 min
Cook: 25 min

4 Servings
1 Non-Starchy Vegetable Per Serving
1 Nutrient-Dense Protein Per Serving
1 Whole-Food Fat Per Serving

Ingredients

- 1 1/2 lbs fresh spinach, cleaned
- 1 lb sole fillet
- 1/2 teaspoon Old Bay Seasoning
- 1 teaspoon extra virgin coconut oil
- 3 green onions, chopped
- 1 garlic clove, crushed

- 2 cups mushrooms, sliced
- 1/2 teaspoon salt
- 1/2 cup chicken broth
- 2 tablespoons coconut flour
- 1/2 cup light cream
- 2 tablespoons parmesan cheese, grated

Directions

1. Preheat oven 375°F.

2. Cook washed spinach with water still clinging over medium-high heat until wilted; drain. When cool enough to handle, gently squeeze out remaining moisture. Finely chop and place in an oiled casserole.

3. Top with the sole filet and sprinkle with Old Bay seasoning.

4. In skillet heat oil; add onions, salt, garlic and mushrooms; sauté for 4 minutes; whisk in coconut flour and slowly add chicken broth and cream stirring constantly for 3-4 minutes until thickened; stir in Parmesan cheese.

5. Spoon over sole.

6. Cover and bake for 20 minutes; uncover and bake another 5 minutes.

Spicy Exotic Fish

Total Time: 37 min
Prep: 30 min
Cook: 7 min

8 Servings
1 Nutrient-Dense Protein Per Serving
1 Whole-Food Fat Per Serving

Ingredients

- 4 lbs filleted red snapper
- 1 1/2 cups freshly squeezed lime juice
- 1 tablespoon curry powder
- 1 tablespoon ground cumin
- 1 tablespoon paprika
- 1 tablespoon allspice

- 1 tablespoon powdered ginger
- 1 tablespoon salt
- 1 tablespoon fresh ground black pepper
- 1 1/2 tablespoons cayenne pepper
- extra virgin coconut oil or cooking spray

Directions

1. Soak the fish in lime juice for 30 minutes in a glass pan or non-corrosive dish.

2. Remove the fish, reserving the juice.

3. Combine the curry powder, cumin, paprika, allspice, ginger, salt, black pepper, and cayenne pepper in a small bowl and stir until well blended.

4. Place each fish fillet on an individual sheet of aluminum foil.

5. Coat each fillet with the spice mixture.

6. Sprinkle a tablespoon of the lime juice over each piece of fish.

7. Wrap each fillet tightly in the foil.

8. Remove the rack from the grill and lightly oil it with extra virgin coconut oil where the fish will placed.

9. Make a fire in the grill and heat the coals until they become somewhat white with ash.

10. Place the fish packets on the grill and cook for 5 minutes.

11. Turn the fish packets and cook for another 3 minutes.

12. Open a packet to see if the fish is done. The flesh should be opaque and the skin should pull away from the flesh; flakiness is usually a sign of overcooking.

STEAMED MUSSELS

Total Time: 20 min   4 Servings
Prep: 15 min   1 Nutrient-Dense Protein Per Serving
Cook: 5 min   1 Whole-Food Fat Per Serving

Ingredients

- 1 (14 1/2 ounce) can chicken broth
- 1/4 cup dry white wine
- 1 teaspoon salt
- 1/4 teaspoon pepper
- 1 1/2 - 2 lbs cleaned fresh mussels

Directions

1. In a large soup kettle, over high heat, combine the chicken broth, wine, salt, and pepper; bring to a boil.

2. Add the mussels, cover, and cook for about 3 to 4 minutes or just until the mussels open.

3. Do not over cook the mussels. Discard any mussels that do not open by themselves.

STEAMED PERUVIAN FISH

Total Time: 20 min   6 Servings
Prep: 5 min   1 Nutrient-Dense Protein Per Serving
Cook: 15 min   1 Whole-Food Fat Per Serving

Ingredients

- 2 tablespoons extra virgin coconut oil
- 1 onion, sliced
- 1 teaspoon garlic, minced
- 2 medium tomatoes, sliced
- 1/4 teaspoon paprika

- 1 teaspoon salt (to taste)
- 1 1/2 lbs white fish fillets
- 1/2 cup dry white wine
- 10 sprigs fresh parsley, leaves only, chopped

Directions

1. Add the onion, garlic, tomatoes, paprika and salt to a large skillet with heated oil.

2. Stir-fry for 2 to 4 minutes.

3. Place the fish fillets over the onion/tomato mixture.

4. Add the wine, cover the skillet, and cook for 5-10 minutes over low heat.

5. Garnish with the parsley.

6. Serve with lemon slices, accompanied by your favorite side dish.

TARRAGON SCALLOPS

Total Time: 15 min
Prep: 5 min
Cook: 10 min

4 Servings
1 Nutrient-Dense Protein Per Serving
1 Whole-Food Fat Per Serving

Ingredients

- 1 1/2 lbs dry sea scallops (the larger type WITHOUT water added)
- 1 garlic clove, minced
- 4 tablespoons unsalted butter

- 1/2-3/4 teaspoon crushed dried tarragon (use twice as much chopped fresh tarragon)
- 1/8 teaspoon paprika
- 1-2 tablespoon shredded parmesan cheese

Directions

1. If some scallops are a lot larger than others, you may want to cut the larger ones in half.

2. Rinse scallops and pat dry with paper towels.

3. In a skillet heat butter over medium-high heat. Add the garlic and lightly sauté for about 1 minute.

4. Add scallops and tarragon. Cook for about 6-7 minutes or until scallops are opaque; turning each once halfway through cooking.

5. Sprinkle with paprika and parmesan cheese and serve immediately.

Tomato-Basil Swordfish

Total Time: 25 min   2 Servings
Prep: 5 min   1 Nutrient-Dense Protein Per Serving
Cook: 20 min   1 Whole-Food Fat Per Serving

Ingredients

- 2 swordfish steaks
- 1 tablespoon extra virgin coconut oil
- salt and pepper
- 1 large ripe tomato, chopped
- 1/2 teaspoon dried basil

Directions

1. Salt and pepper the swordfish steaks.

2. In a sauté pan just large enough to hold the steaks, heat the oil, and quickly brown the swordfish on both sides, but not cooking completely.

3. Remove them from the sauté pan and set aside.

4. In the same pan, add the tomatoes and the basil.

5. Cook for a few minutes, until the tomatoes begin to break down.

6. Return the fish to the pan, covering them with the sauce.

7. Cover the pan, and cook at a low simmer for 4-5 minutes until they are done.

8. Serve!

TROPICAL HALIBUT

Total Time: 48 min
Prep: 40 min
Cook: 8 min

4 Servings
1 Nutrient-Dense Protein Per Serving
1 Whole-Food Fat Per Serving

Ingredients

- 4 (6 -8 ounce) halibut steaks
- 1/2 cup orange juice
- 2 tablespoons extra virgin coconut oil

- 1 1/2 teaspoons cumin
- 1 teaspoon garlic salt
- 1/2 teaspoon coriander

Directions

1. In a 1 gallon resealable food storage plastic bag, combine all ingredients except halibut steaks; shake to mix well.

2. Add halibut, seal bag and turn to coat. Let stand at room temperature for 20 minutes in marinade.

3. Meanwhile heat grill.

4. When ready to grill, remove halibut from bag and discard marinade. Place halibut on gas grill over medium heat or on charcoal grill 4 to 6 inches from medium coals.

5. Cook 8 to 12 mimutes or until fish is no longer translucent in center and flakes easily with fork, turning once.

Note: To broil halibut, place on broiler pan; broil 4 to 6 inches from heat using times above as a guide, turning once.

WHITE FISH PROVENCAL

Total Time: 25 min
Prep: 10 min
Cook: 15 min

4 Servings
1 Non-Starchy Vegetable Per Serving
1 Nutrient-Dense Protein Per Serving
1 Whole-Food Fat Per Serving

Ingredients

- 16 ounces firm white fish fillets, 3/4-1-inch thick
- 3 tablespoons extra virgin coconut oil, divided
- 1/4 teaspoon kosher salt
- 1/4 teaspoon black pepper
- 1/4-1/2 teaspoon onion powder
- 1/4-1/2 teaspoon garlic powder
- 1/2 teaspoon basil leaves, dried and crushed to intensify flavor
- 1/2 teaspoon thyme leaves, dried and crushed to intensify flavor
- 8 ounces stewed tomatoes, drained of most liquid
- 1/2 cup olive (Kalamata, Green, or Black Olives)
- 1/4 cup white wine

Directions

1. Preheat oven to 375 degrees.

2. Place fish fillets in an oven safe baking dish.

3. Drizzle 1-1/2 tablespoon extra virgin coconut oil over fish. Rub oil on both sides and Salt & Pepper.

4. Sprinkle fish with Onion and Garlic Powders, Basil and Thyme herbs.

5. Top with a 1-1/2 heaping tablespoon of Stewed Tomatoes per fillet

6. Pit and slice Olives into halves or quarters and sprinkle on top of tomatoes (Kalamata is delicious in this recipe).

7. Splash the tops of tomatoes & olives with White Wine and drizzle the remaining extra virgin coconut oil.

8. Bake with a foil tent for 15 minutes or until fish is white and flakey.

So Much To Look Forward To...

You will learn much more about this as we start your personal weight-loss plan together in your free half-day Masterclass (reserve your seat at SANESeminar.com), but here are a few key reminders as you're getting started on your SANE journey.

SANE eating is a lifelong, enjoyable, sustainable, simple, and delicious way of eating. **It is not a repackaging of the unsustainable calorie counting diets that failed you.**

I know you understand this already—otherwise you wouldn't be here—but please keep in mind that since SANE isn't a calorie counting diet, you will not suffer through the same calorie counting tools and resources that failed you in the past. For example, **memorizing endless food lists and following unrealistic minute-by-minute meal plans aren't just a pain— they cannot work in the real world**, and they cannot work long term.

Life is crazy. Things happen. And heck, people have different tastes in food, so while minute-by-minute "eat exactly this right now no matter what" endless lists might make for good reality TV, if they worked in the real world, you would have already met your goals. **To get a different result (long-term fat loss and robust health), you MUST take a different approach.** That's what you will find here.

If you approach your new SANE life calmly, gradually, and with the next 30 years in mind rather than the next 30 days, **you will learn the underlying principles that enable you to make the SANE choices easily—forever**.

Think of your new approach as the difference between memorizing the sum of every possible combination of numbers versus learning the underlying principles of how addition works. Once you understand addition, lists and memorization aren't necessary as you know what to do with any combination of numbers—forever.

The same thing applies with food. Once you understand the new science of SANE eating, **you will know exactly what to eat (and what to avoid) everywhere you go—forever—without any lists** or any memorization.

This new approach changes everything and will forever free you from all the confusing and conflicting weight-loss information you've been told. So please allow me to congratulate you on coming to the life-changing realization that **to get different results than you've gotten in the past, you must take a different approach than you used in the past!**

The great news is that when you combine a calm, gradual, long-term, and progress vs. perfection mindset with your scientifically proven SANE tools, program, and coaching, you are **guaranteed to burn belly fat, boost energy, and enjoy an unstoppable sense of self-confidence!**

Your new SANE lifestyle has helped over 100,000 people in over 37 countries burn fat and boost health *long-term....*and it will do the same for you if you let it and trust it.

Thank you for taking the road less travelled...it will make all the difference!

SANEly and Gratefully,

Jonathan Bailor | SANE Founder, NYTimes Bestselling Author, and soon...your personal weight-loss coach

P.S. Over the years I have found that our most successful members, the ones who have lost 60, 70, even 100 pounds... and kept it off... are the ones who start their personal weight-loss plan on...

our FREE half-day Masterclass. It's your best opportunity to fall in love with the SANE lifestyle, learn exactly how to start making the simple changes that lead to dramatic body transformations, and get introduced to your new SANE family. Be sure to reserve your spot at http://SANESeminar.com.

Please Don't Lose Your Seat at the FREE Masterclass Seminar!

Reserve your spot now so we can start your perfect personalized weight-loss plan. Space is limited and fills-up quickly. Reserve your spot now so you don't miss out!

Yes! I want to reserve my spot now at SANESeminar.com

About the Author: Jonathan Bailor is a New York Times bestselling author and internationally recognized natural weight loss expert who specializes in using modern science and technology to simplify health. Bailor has collaborated with top scientists for more than 10 years to analyze and apply over 1,300 studies. His work has been endorsed by top doctors and scientists from Harvard Medical School, Johns' Hopkins, The Mayo Clinic, The Cleveland Clinic, and UCLA.

Bailor is the founder of SANESolution.com and serves as the CEO for the wellness technology company Yopti®. He authored the New York Times and USA Today bestselling book *The Calorie Myth*, hosts a popular syndicated health radio show *The SANE Show*, and blogs on *The Huffington Post*. Additionally, Bailor has registered over 25 patents, spoken at Fortune 100 companies and TED conferences for over a decade, and served as a Senior Program Manager at Microsoft where he helped create Nike+ Kinect Training and XBox Fitness.

Get Everything You Need To Burn Fat and Prepare Delicious Meals at the SANE Store

Fat-Burning Flour

Mood-Boosting Chocolate Powder

Clean Pea Protein

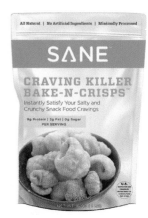

Craving Killer Bake-N-Crisps

Slimming Sugar Substitute

Clean Whey Protein

Vanilla Almond Meal Bars

Craving Killer Chocolate Truffle

 No Added Sugar

 100% Natural

 Gluten Free

 No GMO's

 No Dairy

No Soy

SANE™ Find all of these EXCLUSIVE tools, plus over 100 other fat-burning SANE products to help you and your family look and feel your best!

Visit Today: Store.SANESolution.com

Printed in Great Britain
by Amazon